Options For The Teaching Of English

Freshman Composition

Edited by
Jasper P. Neel

Published by The Modern Language Association of America
62 Fifth Avenue, New York, New York 10011

Contents

Contents

Introduction

For more than a century, American colleges have designed, redesigned, eliminated, reinstated, required, and suggested writing programs of every conceivable size and kind. In the 1970s the search for a workable composition program has been unusually intense, and the essays in this book indicate the wide variety of composition programs currently in operation at all types of colleges—two-year, four-year, rural, urban, public, private, graduate, undergraduate. If there is anything that distinguishes the 1970s from other periods in the history of American college composition programs, it is that teachers and administrators have begun to see the teaching of composition as an end in itself, not a temporary assignment on the way to bigger and better things.

The only way to show *all* the options for teaching composition would be to describe the composition program at every college in the nation, but the essays in this book do offer a cross section of the various approaches currently in use. To be sure, there are major disagreements among the writers: while some argue that composition is at the heart of the English discipline and should be the foundation of each English department, others argue that it is no more essential to the English department than to any other department and that it should be extra-departmental; while some describe very elaborate remedial programs, others argue that *remediation* is not a meaningful term; while some take pride in the pluralism of their programs and argue that housing numerous approaches to teaching composition within a single department is healthy, others take pride in the department-wide systems of teaching composition they have developed; while some argue that composition must be taught by progressing from sentence to paragraph to essay, others argue that the only way to teach writing is to require whole essays right from the beginning; while some argue that programs should be "product" oriented, others argue that they should be "process" oriented, and still others argue that they should be both.

The points on which the writers disagree, however, are not nearly as important as the points on which they agree. All agree that composition teachers must base their teaching on some theory of how writing is learned and how it can be taught. All agree that composition teachers must respect their work and themselves, that composition cannot be taught well by teachers who see it as drudge-work and who receive second-rate professional and financial rewards for their efforts. All agree that every college must design a program that motivates students to learn to write, that students must see some connection between their personal aspirations and their ability to write. Finally, all agree that the only way anyone ever learns to write is by writing a great deal for a clearly defined audience.

The institutional data recorded at the beginning of each essay reveal nothing startling. Even in 1976 most composition courses in most colleges were not taught by members of the professorial ranks (assistant, associate, and full professors); at all but one of the Ph.D.-granting institutions represented in this book, for example, more than eighty-five percent of the composition courses were taught by graduate students. Even so, almost every composition program accounts for a substantial percentage, usually about fifty percent, of the total effort of the department that houses the program.

Ten of the eighteen programs can be described as traditional. That is, they are designed (in all but one case, required) for freshmen, and though they serve the entire campus, they are housed in an English department. The Wyoming program serves as a good introduction to this group because the history of required composition at Wyoming is very much like that of writing programs across America. The other nine traditional programs show how various colleges in various places have adapted an almost universal requirement to their own needs. In the East, at City College and Queens College of the City University of New York, the English departments were compelled to deal with the "new students" who enrolled after the establishment of open admissions. In the South, the University of Virginia and Reynolds Community College—two very different colleges in the same state—meet the needs of widely differing student bodies in different ways. At Reynolds, an urban, two-year college, the English department has developed a very careful system of placing students at various points in the program; it has also extended the writing program into businesses in the community at large. At Virginia, the department relies on small classes—limited to eighteen—and a workshop approach. In the Southwest, the University of Texas at Austin and Arizona State University operate programs based on writing theories developed by members of their respective faculties, yet still make provisions for the ethnic groups that live in their part of the country. In the Midwest, Missouri and Ohio State operate large programs staffed almost exclusively with graduate students in English. At Missouri the core of the program is the system of training teaching assistants; at Ohio State the department relies on a published set of minimum standards and an emphasis on the "process" of writing. In the Pacific Northwest, the University of Washington offers three different programs: a product-oriented reading/writing course, a process-oriented course graded credit/no credit, and a series of courses for students who are not prepared for college work.

The eight nontraditional programs have been labeled nontraditional for a variety of reasons. In four of the eight institutions, the writing requirement is not the responsibility of the English department. The University of Iowa has operated a rhetoric department for thirty years. Although it has only ten full-time faculty members and ninety percent of its courses are taught by members of other departments, the rhetoric department itself is completely autonomous. The program is somewhat unusual in that its courses include not only writing but also reading, speaking, and listening. The writing program that will be instituted at the University of Southern California in 1978 will also be separated from other departments, although, like the Iowa program, it will draw its staff from several other departments. The most distinctive feature of the Southern California program is that students will not be "placed" at all: all classes will have students at all stages in the program from the first semester through the third; the teacher will keep track of each student's progress toward completion of the requirement. At Central College in Iowa responsibility for teaching "basic skills" has been shifted from the English department to the entire faculty of the college; each department designates some of its courses as skills courses, and each department certifies that its majors can read, write, and speak adequately. At Michigan State University, students can meet the composition requirement by taking courses offered by four different units within the university; as a result, the English department operates a very small freshman composition program and a much larger, elective sophomore composition program. In collaboration with the natural sciences departments, the English department also offers a year-long "science writing" program.

The other four nontraditional programs are dramatically nontraditional. The Dallas County Community College District has developed a district-wide televised composition program. The experimental Small College of California State College, Dominguez Hills, has developed a "writing adjunct" program that links writing instruction to a wide variety of courses in a number of departments. At Brown University, which assumes that all the students it admits have already learned to write effectively, members of the English department have developed a special program for those who, after being admitted, reveal that they need help with writing. Finally, the humanities department in the University of Michigan's College of Engineering, after having abolished the freshman composition requirement entirely, has instituted a required *senior*-level rhetoric program.

To be sure, there are many good composition programs in American colleges. The eighteen represented in this book were chosen not because they are the "best" but because they offer an overview of the ways different institutions deal with the teaching of writing.

Jasper P. Neel

The Freshman Writing Program at the University of Wyoming

John Warnock, Director of Freshman English, and
Tilly Eggers, Director of the Writing Center

Department responsible for the composition program   English
Full-time faculty in the department   37
Enrollment policies
    Maximum Enrollment   26
    Minimum Enrollment   10
    Average Enrollment   24
Staffing
    Percentage of freshman composition courses taught by graduate students   44
    Percentage taught by part-time faculty (excluding graduate students)   15
    Percentage taught by full-time instructors or lecturers   30
    Percentage taught by assistant, associate, and full professors   11
Program size
    Number of students enrolled in the freshman composition program in the fall term of 1976   1,719
    Number of sections of freshman composition offered in the fall term of 1976   75
    Number of sections at all levels—literature, composition, film, graduate, undergraduate, etc.—offered by the department in the fall term of 1976   129

In this brief account of the freshman English program at the University of Wyoming, we shall try to reveal the motives of the program. To do so, we must go a little beyond bare statements of purpose and practice. In this case there is something to be learned by beginning at the beginning:

History

The University of Wyoming is a land-grant college founded under the Morrill Act of 1862. Though the Morrill Act was intended to give special encouragement to "agriculture and the mechanic arts," the university's first college was Liberal Arts, and, for most of its history, the university has shown a commitment to the liberal arts as the foundation of higher education.

In the beginning, there were seven faculty, forty-two students, and no English department. There was, however, the following four-year requirement, appearing in the 1891–92 catalog under the heading *Rhetoricals*:

> The students in Freshman, Sophomore and Junior classes of the College of Liberal Arts and students in the Junior and Senior year of the Technical Schools will be divided into four divisions for Rhetorical work, and will come on performance once a month, either in essay, declamation, debate or oration. This oratorical work will be in charge of the faculty of the College of Liberal Arts.
>
> The Seniors will be required to deliver three orations before the faculty and students during the Senior year.

A special feature of the university in these early years was a two-year preparatory course, separate from the four-year course, designed for students whose high school performance was weak. Students in the prep course took "English Analysis" their first year and "English Composition" their second year. This looks a bit like freshman English; whatever it was, it preceded the creation of the English department by some years.

In the regular college course in those early days, all students took French, German, and Latin in their first year; "Rhetoric" in their second; "Philosophy of Rhetoric or Literary Criticism" in their third; and "Oratory" in the senior year. By 1907, however, the college requirement in oratory had been dropped, and for the first time a description of a department of English appeared in the catalog:

> The work in this department falls naturally into three divisions: Composition, Public Speaking and Oratory, Literature and Philology.
>
> The various studies that comprise the first of these groups, from their great significance in the daily business of the world, receive the weight of attention.

There appears to have been a university-wide requirement in freshman English in 1908, and by 1912 the English department had become the largest on campus. A year of freshman English has been required without interruption since 1908, and in 1977, with twenty-seven professorial faculty, ten full-time instructors, six part-time instructors, and eighteen teaching assistants in a university faculty of 750, the English department was still the largest. We do not know what proportion of the department's enrollment in 1908 was attributable to freshman English, but in the fall of 1977 the figure was sixty-three percent, or 1,820 students.

Thus it seems that, at the University of Wyoming at least, freshman English has always had some importance, even before the English department came to exist. We also see that some of the ambivalence English departments may feel toward freshman English is here built in. Freshman English seems to have begun as something needed by those not yet ready for the college course (and the rhetoricals), but it continued as something the new English department declared worthy of the attention it received because of its "great significance in the daily business of the world."

We turn now to some of the university's variations on the theme of freshman English. Some of them have a modern or, perhaps, timeless ring. For example, in 1916, eight years after the course became a university-wide requirement, it was described as follows:

> The purpose of this course is to develop ability in thinking and corresponding ability in writing and speaking. The aim is not so much literary as practical. As a requirement for all Freshmen, . . . it is planned to have as much direct application as possible to each individual's major study. Modern style and diction [are] studied from selected periodicals.

A substantial change from this "not-so-much-literary as practical," no-nonsense approach occurred in 1926, though it was a change neither to "composition for literature majors" nor to nonsense. The description of freshman English for 1926 read:

> Analysis of the student's own language habits with a view to development. Consideration of language and literature in their relation to mental growth. Training in the technique of observation, record [sic] and organization of the facts of our language and literature experiences. Language and literature considered as normal functions to be cultivated, and composition as a means of organization and establishment of attitudes.

This surprisingly "modern" language was that of the new head of the English department, Vincil Coulter, who kept the headship and this rubric for almost twenty years. In 1945 Coulter's successor, Wilson Clough, faced with the great influx of returning veterans, embarked on a new program which he described as "pragmatic rather than inspirational." The university had switched from the semester to the quarter system, and the freshman English course emphasized grammar in the first quarter; exposition, argumentation, and rhetorical types in the second quarter; and literary types in the third quarter. When the university returned to semesters in 1955, it planned that the study of "literary types" should occupy only one third of the year's course. Literature quickly came to occupy all of the second semester, however, and the second semester came to be called "Introduction to Literary Types." In the 1960s the course name was changed to "Freshman Composition" to answer the charge that the course was one in "humanities," and not "composition."

The shape of Wyoming's two semesters of freshman English at present resembles in many respects the shape of the course that emerged after 1955, which is also the shape of many of the courses Thomas Wilcox surveyed in *The Anatomy of College English*.[1] But before going on to describe that shape and the theory that informs and criticizes it, we feel we must try to characterize the place occupied by the principal concern of the course—writing—in the University of Wyoming and in its English department.

Writing in the University

In the spring of 1977, we undertook a survey of the students, the faculty, and the heads of departments to discover a number of things, the most important of which were, perhaps, how much writing seems to count in the university, what counts, and when it counts. Our hypothesis was and is that whatever we found to be true of the University of Wyoming would also be true of many other colleges and universities. This is not the place to report extensively on the findings. But some results are interesting and relevant.[2]

First, 70.9% of the faculty responding felt that a person's performance as a writer would affect *career* success heavily or very heavily, while only 48.9% felt that it affected the *academic* success of their undergraduates heavily or very heavily. Students' opinions ran closely parallel to the faculty's in this respect. The fact that faculty and students think writing counts more in one's job than in school is, we feel, a little startling. It suggests a state of affairs in the university not at all easy to justify, a state of affairs that would, furthermore, necessarily inhibit the teaching and learning of composition in freshman English classes, whatever the other problems might be.

Second, while 80.3% of freshmen responding think systematic instruction in writing is most useful in the freshman year (many think it would be useful in more than one year), it is clear that students do little writing as freshmen and sophomores and that most of their writing is done when they are juniors and seniors.

Third, we observe a variance among faculty and students as to how well students write. While 12.8% of faculty think undergraduates in their field write "quite poorly," 48.3% think they write "rather poorly," 29.1% think they write adequately, and only 5.9% think they write well or very well; in contrast, 40.4% of students think they are "good" writers and only 7.2% think they are "poor" writers.

Fourth, department heads reported that there was a great deal of variation among their teachers in both the amount of writing and (somewhat less) the kind of writing assigned.

Finally, students responded much more positively to the question "How much did you learn in freshman English?" than to the question "How much did freshman English help you in other courses?"

We may tentatively conclude the following: Writing seems not to count for much in the student's immediate academic environment. Thus, we cannot expect much of what is sometimes called extrinsic motivation. The possibility

—in fact, the likelihood—exists that there is something to be learned in freshman English that is important to students as writers but not as majors in most other fields. If we abandoned writing in general as our concern and took up instead a service role, we might find that we have no role at all.

Writing in the Department

Today, though forty-four percent of the courses are taught by teaching assistants (89% by teaching assistants and instructors), all professors are committed to teaching freshman English once every three semesters or so. Nor are new faculty hired unless they show some interest and ability in teaching writing.

Our graduate program (M.A. only) has recently added to its usual plans for literary study and creative writing a plan that includes a course in teaching college composition. The department does have a faculty member appointed jointly to the Education College, but to date it has paid little attention to the requirements of writing teachers in the secondary schools.

The Theory

The commitments set out here are those of the two authors, the directors of the freshman English program and the writing center; the theory set out here informs our efforts to evaluate syllabuses and textbooks, to train teachers, and to answer questions about what ought to be going on in the composition classroom. Though our theoretical commitments do not dictate any particular program, they do give us an attitude that is likely to tell in the search for curriculum and pedagogy, and they also enable us to say no to certain proposals. Needless to say, not everyone who teaches composition at the university is interested in the theoretical questions (or the research bearing on them). Not everyone has read the works to be cited, nor could they be expected to accept all of the arguments expressed in the works if they did read them.

On this occasion the theory must be presented without much clarification and with little attempt at justification. We recognize that theory must be put to the test and also that there has been little effort to systematize theories of writing and of teaching writing. We also recognize the need to make explicit the theory implied by our practice, the better to criticize both. Here it seems best to refer to some major theoretical statements and some of their consequences for practice, trusting the curious or puzzled reader to fill in the gaps as necessary.

Kenneth Burke's *A Grammar of Motives*[3] could provide the background for this whole discussion. We see writing, in Burke's terms, as a dramatism, as neither product nor process, but as an *action* involving in all "real" cases an actor, an act, an agency, a purpose, and a scene. This commitment causes us to say no to any scheme (in textbook or syllabus) that fails to acknowledge the full eventfulness of writing.

James Kinneavy's *A Theory of Discourse*[4] classifies texts according to aim.

As such, it is not directly concerned with giving an account of the full event-fulness of writing. Nevertheless, it gives a map of the domain of discourse that makes us say no to programs that offer to teach students to write without acknowledging that the logic, organization, and style of writing will vary according to the primary aim of the discourse. It also makes us say no to theories that purport to classify the kinds of discourse according to a trun-cated nineteenth-century faculty psychology, as description, narration, exposi-tion, and argumentation on the grounds that such a scheme conflates mode and aim and is thus fundamentally incoherent.

Young, Becker, and Pike's *Rhetoric: Discovery and Change*[5] gives us writ-ing as a process of inquiry, inviting us to consider not just the means by which a writer's intention may be realized relative to his reader but the means by which we may learn to discover, articulate, and solve ill-defined problems. This commitment makes us say no to programs that offer to split off "invention" from writing, and no to programs that would make rhetoric the merely dec-orative (or anti-decorative) art it is sometimes taken to be.

The Development of Writing Abilities (11–18), by James Britton, et al., and James Moffet's *Teaching the Universe of Discourse*[6] support our com-mitment to the centrality of development (or acquisition), not learning, in "learning" to write. This makes us say no to simple deductive teaching, to programs that take as primary the teaching of rules of grammar, paragraph structure, of the essay as needing an introduction, a body and a conclusion, and so on. We recognize that this kind of learning has its place, but we believe that it is a much more limited place than is usually believed, even when it comes to "learning" the requirements of standard English. This theoretical commitment impels us to search for scenes in which writing may be naturally and rationally acted out. Here Burke steps in again to help us see that these scenes are to be imagined not simply in terms of assignments for the classroom but also in terms of the symbolic acts that constitute the university and the society at large. Nor are they to be seen as related in merely a linear fashion, but as part of a complex and redundant dialectic.

The Program

We may now describe the university's program in freshman English. The ends of the first-semester course are described in the department's "Syllabus of Suggestions and Policies" as follows:

> [In the first-semester course] students are called upon to prac-tice writing and to consider some conceptual matters that bear upon the practice of writing. These conceptual matters include principles of logic, organization and style related to: the writer's presentation of self, the writer's address to the audience, the writer's representation of the world, the potentialities of the writer's medium, namely, the English language.
>
> At the end of [the course], students should be able to pro-duce writing which is informed throughout by a sense of vitality and purpose. Minimal expectations are that a student's writing: 1) will be responsive to course assignments; 2) will not, when it is

inappropriate, deviate substantially from the conventions of correct usage observed generally in formal written discourse with respect to such matters as spelling, noun and verb agreement, punctuation, and the sentence unit; 3) will move from sentence to sentence and paragraph to paragraph in a way that is unconfusing to the reader, producing in the end a sense of coherence in the writing taken as a whole; 4) will exhibit a sense of the requirements of logic and validity of reference in writing that concerns itself with representing the world.

Students must have a grade of C in [the first-semester course] to go on to [the second-semester course], and an inability to meet any of the minimal expectations set out above is sufficient grounds for a grade of less than C.

[The second-semester course differs from the first-semester course in that] the conceptual matters bearing upon writing are presented largely through an examination of literary works. . . . [S]tudents . . . will not be asked to produce final critical evaluations of the literary works they read. Instead, they will be asked to engage in open-minded and careful exploration of the works, and to produce writing that shows tact, honest and straightforward inquiry, and exact and careful observation. They will be asked, in other words, for no more and no less than should be brought to an investigation of a complex human problem in real life. In this respect, students will be learning skills applicable far beyond strictly literary studies.

Each three-credit-hour semester requires six thousand words of edited writing (with the proviso that some kind of writing ought to be going on almost all the time), and a project causing the students to use the library is required in the second semester.

There are "honors" sections of freshman English, taken by about ten percent of the students in the course each semester. This ten percent used to be identified solely through ACT test scores. When, in 1974, the UW administration interpreted "open-door" to mean that no tests could be required as a condition of admission, we found that most of the students who would have qualified for the "honors" course still took the test, so we can still use the test to find students for the course. Also, faculty advisers (every student must have one at UW) are asked to enroll likely students who haven't taken the test.

Our rationale for these "honors" classes is complex. We do not believe that people who do well on the ACT test, or any other test that measures mastery of the rules and conventions of standard English, will necessarily be better writers than those who cannot show such mastery. In fact, they will often be much more insistent than the "regular" students in attempting to reduce "good" writing to "correct" writing. They are likely to overuse rules and to be unable to acquire the habits and attitudes of genuine inquiry. The separation of overusers of rules from those who do not yet show mastery of the rules and conventions of standard English makes some sense to us, though it has the ironic effect of making the "honors" sections into a special kind of remedial class. We also feel that students of real talent and developed ability may profit most from a course which emphasizes inquiry rather than competence.

We have at present no remedial course. From its beginnings, the university has made efforts to remediate with required courses, as in the college prep course described above. The last effort of this kind was a one-semester, no-credit, two-tries-only course, phased out in the early sixties on the argument that there was no longer a need for it. Since 1974, the university has interpreted "open-door" to mean that students cannot be required to take remedial courses before taking the regular freshman English course. This prevents us from doing what we wouldn't do if we could. We do not want to permit the question of remediation to be separated from the question of development. We do not want the goals of remediation to be reduced to learning the rules and conventions of standard English. And we do not want the students, the teachers, or the legislators to imagine that remediation is to be achieved in an isolated course, required or otherwise.

In the fall of 1977, the English department opened a writing center for all students, at all levels. The center grew out of three premises: (1) that the university has a moral obligation to offer (but not to require) a real means of assistance to the students it admits who are likely to fail freshman English because of inadequate educational background; (2) that there is no basis for believing that remedial courses could provide this assistance for an acceptable percentage of the students required to take the courses; (3) that the department and the university need a place where writing can be taught within context for students (and others) better than it can be in the regular courses. Teaching within context includes such matters as (a) cooperating with other departments—other faculty members leading mini-courses in such special kinds of writing as research reports, computer language, professional editing, and the like; (b) training teachers of writing through practical experience and through a library of materials; (c) conducting research and discussions of current developments in the theory of composition. An individual in need of special assistance in writing can begin to solve his or her problems by defining them in these contexts.

Training Teachers

The University of Wyoming freshman English program does not have a daily or weekly or six-weekly syllabus. We feel that in our situation such a syllabus would not be workable, even if we thought one desirable. Instead the freshman English office offers a general syllabus of suggestions and policies, and it maintains a departmental library which we have tried to stock with all current texts produced by the market along with a selection of the more important theoretical and empirical research.

Each semester a textbook committee, composed of three faculty and a representative of the teaching assistants, meets to recommend texts for the next semester. The list is annotated and several options indicated. If teaching assistants wish to depart from the titles on the list, they must get the approval of the Director of Freshman English.

Although, as must be the case in all English departments, there are faculty with no special training in teaching composition, our efforts to train teachers are directed primarily at our teaching assistants. We recognize (1) that not all TAs are especially interested in writing and (2) that many TAs will get so involved in their teaching that their course work will suffer. So we urge, but do not require, all TAs to take the graduate course in teaching writing. We require them to attend what we call colloquia, which meet for seven hours during registration and then about once every two weeks for the rest of the semester. Here we deal with certain crucial administrative and pedagogical matters, but we also try to respond to requests by the TAs themselves. We always have a couple of grading sessions. TAs are assigned faculty mentors who are expected to check on their grading practices and to help in other ways when possible. The amount of help given varies with the mentor.

Conclusion

We may conclude with a brief list of some issues that are part of the present scene and that seem to the authors to contain the seeds of future change in the writing program at the University of Wyoming: How may we achieve an acceptable reliability in the final grades for freshman English? How may the relationships between reading and writing be made to inform more fruitfully the English department's curriculum? What is the relation of the department's work to English in the secondary schools? Should the department, building upon its current offerings, develop an M.A. program in rhetoric?

Notes

[1] Thomas W. Wilcox, *The Anatomy of College English* (San Francisco: Jossey-Bass Publishers, 1973).

[2] The survey was conducted with the assistance of Robert S. Cochran, Department of Statistics, University of Wyoming. For further information, write to the authors: English Department, University of Wyoming, Laramie, Wyoming.

[3] Kenneth Burke, *A Grammar of Motives* (New York: Prentice-Hall, 1945).

[4] James Kinneavy, *A Theory of Discourse* (Englewood Cliffs, N.J.: Prentice-Hall, 1971).

[5] Richard Young, Alton Becker, Kenneth Pike, *Rhetoric: Discovery and Change* (New York: Harcourt Brace Jovanovich, 1970).

[6] James Britton *et al.*, *The Development of Writing Abilities (11–18)* (London: Macmillan Educational, 1968); James Moffett, *Teaching the Universe of Discourse* (Boston: Houghton Mifflin, 1968).

Basic Writing at the City College of the City University of New York

Blanche Skurnick, Director of Basic Writing

Department responsible for the composition program   English
Full-time faculty in the department   75
Enrollment policies
    Maximum Enrollment   27
    Minimum Enrollment   15
    Average Enrollment   23
Staffing
    Percentage of freshman composition courses taught by part-time faculty (excluding graduate students)   5
    Percentage taught by full-time instructors or lecturers   15
    Percentage taught by assistant, associate, and/or full professors   60
    Percentage taught by full-time members of departments other than English   20
Program size
    Number of students enrolled in the freshman composition program in the fall term of 1976   2,873
    Number of sections of freshman composition offered in the fall term of 1976   125
    Number of sections at all levels—literature, composition, film, graduate, undergraduate, etc.—offered by the department in the fall term of 1976   233

As enrollments shrink and competition for students heats, administrators at CCNY cast cold eyes on the basic writing program. They question placements, call for ever-larger classes, and press professors of history and classics into the basic writing classroom. For from their point of view, few students really need composition: the poor writer will never learn to write, and the good learner doesn't have to be taught how. Nonetheless, most students continue to place into the basic writing program and to struggle through the sequence.

History

In 1965 the SEEK (Search for Education Elevation and Knowledge) program was established at CCNY to enable students who would have been excluded under existing criteria on the basis of their grades to prepare for college through a series of special courses, among them composition courses, incorporating college work and remedial work, and augmented by tutoring and professional counseling. As SEEK was getting under way, the rest of the student body were demanding greater freedom to select their courses and a greater voice in the content of those courses. Requirements in liberal arts were loosened in response to these demands, and in 1969 the two-semester freshman composition course requirement was dropped. In its place a writing proficiency examination was introduced, and students were required to pass it to graduate. In the same year, students in the SEEK program demanded that they be matriculated into the college as regular students. They wanted the courses they were taking to generate credit in keeping with the hours they spent in them and on them, and they wanted the opportunity they had had to enter college to be extended to all students who completed high school in New York City. To meet these demands, the Board of Higher Education began open admissions in the fall of 1970, five years earlier than planned.

Having dropped the composition requirement, the college adopted the on-campus SEEK model for remedial composition for all entering students. It provided for placement in one of three courses or exemption from all based on writing skill demonstrated on a placement examination. Students placing in the first or second course in the sequence were required to complete the sequence.

Structure of the Program

The three-semester basic writing program begun in September of 1970 drew heavily on the SEEK model for its theoretical base as well as for its structure. After five years of teaching students who had done little writing how to write formal discourse in standard English, and of monitoring their progress, and of experimenting with different teaching strategies and subject matter, our composition teachers had arrived at a pragmatic pedagogy. Though highly individual approaches remained (and still do, as will be seen), the basic writing faculty felt that they had sound answers to some of the large theoretical questions always debated at conferences on college writing. Though everyone understood that teaching grammar does not improve composition, no one felt that the syntactic features of the many social and regional dialects our students reproduced in their writing could be ignored. Few felt that these features would disappear as students read or as they sat in class listening to their classmates. Some of us debated the degree of in-class attention that ought to be given to "errors," but no one denied that they were critical. Accordingly, the sentence was made the subject of the first level of basic writing, English 1. Poor control of the sentence placed a student in English 1 no matter how well he managed other prose features.

Nor was there any question that we must teach formal writing: analysis, proposition, and synthesis—requiring the writer to gather and organize information on subjects outside his personal experience, to pose questions about it, and to generalize from it. Everyone had observed that most students write description and narration better than they do exposition and argument and that they control subjects within their experience better than abstractions or information new to them. So the paragraph and the short expository essay were adopted as the subjects of English 2, the second level of the sequence.

Our aim in SEEK had been to enable students to manage their college work successfully: not to teach them to love to write, not to introduce them to literature (though literature was often required reading in the courses), not to "get them through" the proficiency examination. The aim seemed no less sound under open admissions: make able writers of them. Thus we retained the third course in the SEEK sequence, on the techniques of research and the research paper form, because the research paper is a common course requirement. We knew too that students who entered the sequence at English 1 or English 2 would continue to need close supervision of their writing. Designed to meet these two different ends, English 3 is listed as a quasi-remedial course. English 1 and 2, like their SEEK precursors, are designated remedial.

In the transition from the SEEK model to the basic writing sequence, the first level, a six-hour course in the SEEK sequence, was reduced to four; the second level remained four hours, and the third level three. Class sizes were increased from a maximum of fifteen students per section to eighteen in English 1, twenty in English 2, and twenty-three in English 3 (these numbers are now slightly higher). Budget restrictions caused these increases, but we have been able to maintain supervised tutoring in a writing center for SEEK students, and basic writing courses still feature individual teacher-student conferences several times a semester. Salvaging these has been important. An informed and experienced audience is essential to a writer's development. In tutoring sessions and in conferences, student papers are read and discussed line by line, giving the student a sense of the choices he has made, the questions he has raised, and the impression he has achieved. The most productive work done in the basic writing program is done in these conferences.

Placement

In September of 1970, fifty percent of the entering class were admitted under open admissions criteria, and fifty percent were students who would have been admitted under the old criteria. It was assumed, then (at least by some administrators), that basic writing would serve half these entrants, and that the other half would not need these courses. But since 1970, no fewer than ninety percent of each entering class have placed into basic writing. Of these, one quarter regularly place into English 1, nearly half into English 2, and the remainder into English 3. The procedures for placement have changed somewhat in the intervening years, but these percentages have not.

The placement examination has two parts: an objective short-answer test and an essay question. Originally the objective test used was one developed at City College by Mina Shaughnessy, who had designed the SEEK courses and was then Director of Basic Writing. When this test became too expensive to score, it was replaced by the Cooperative English Test, which was succeeded by the Stanford Reading Test. The objective test is given to reduce the number of essays that have to be read to make initial placements in basic writing (entering classes have been as large as 3,500 under open admissions). Objective test scores are correlated with placements made by essay readings to establish objective test-score ranges for placement in each of the three courses of the sequence. A group of readers in the English department then reads only the essays of those students whose objective test scores fall within overlapping ranges—usually about half of those tested. Because only half of the essays have been read, initial placement is tentative; when classes convene, teachers secure writing samples immediately, and then adjust the placements of those students whose essays differ in structure, depth, or fluency from those written by the rest of the class—which, in English 2 and 3, is composed of initial placements and students moving through the sequence, and so provides a meaningful comparison.

English 1 placements are typically students who mismanage inflections, sentence boundaries, tense consistency, and the like. Placements in English 2 are students who write standard English but don't manage paragraph structure, logic, wording, generalization, or elaboration effectively. These students haven't written much, though some have strong high-school averages. Placements in English 3 resemble pre-open admissions freshmen. But unlike their predecessors, who were required to take a full year of composition, students placed in English 3 are advised, but not required, to take the course. Those placed in English 2 also stand at a disadvantage, since they are taking a "remedial" course and will take a quasi-remedial course but are given no more time to complete freshman composition, such as it is, than was given to their predecessors—who in addition enjoyed a course without stigma.

Teaching Strategies and Guidelines

Most of the teaching strategies in basic writing are designed to transform student writing from obstacle to instrument as quickly as possible. Strategies vary, deriving from what individual instructors feel are primary enabling skills: ability to perceive what treatment the question or topic demands; ability to predict audience questions; ability to structure information logically; ability to perceive the nuances of words; ability to read one's own words critically; ability to get started, and so forth. These notions fall into two camps, structural and semantic. The structural strategists teach introduction-body-conclusion, the five-paragraph theme, description, narration, modes of argument, and so forth, on the theory that teaching the devices of development will enable students to write effectively. The semantic strategists hold that development springs from ideas. They teach by throwing out questions (*Can an infant be guilty?*) and propositions (*No one is guilty. Everyone is guilty.*), and by exposing the writing in its planning stages and in its final form to group response. With the exception of new faculty, who are asked to structure their courses from basic writing syllabuses on file, individual instructors devise their own syllabuses and select their own texts in accord with whichever of these fundamental skills they feel is essential to develop others. But several practices are common. Most instructors have students revise each essay at least once, and most instructors present models—formats, formulas, or essays—themselves, of the kinds of essays they ask students to write.

In 1973 the director of the program and a committee of teachers set down guidelines for all basic writing courses, outlining the general course content at each level and the criteria for passing from one level to the next. The guidelines stipulate that each basic writing student should write a total of ten thousand words per semester, in the form of weekly themes, in-class essays, revisions, summaries, and journals. They also stipulate what the student should have learned by the time he completes the course: how to concentrate on meaning, how to proofread for error, how to determine the degree of specificity required by his statements, how to sustain a thesis in a long paper, etc. Teachers are free to choose how to work within these guidelines. Some have developed writing workshops, in which there is little lecturing. Students write and edit in class, and the course content is the writing produced. One has a peer-teaching enterprise, in which students present the various units of the course (usually English 1) to the rest of the class, learning to research and to organize information as they learn the information. Others have developed proofreading schemes that require students to recognize sentence structures in which errors occur often, learn how these structures behave, and read for these structures in their writing. One of these techniques uses the principles of sentence combining to teach recognition; another uses perception exercises. One instructor has a revision scheme in which students annotate the paragraphs they write and redraft from the annotations; another revision scheme calls for revision from a list of inferences drawn from the first draft.

None of these schemes derives from any single theory of rhetoric or of learning. Most are a precious essence of many trials; but instructors have selected ideas from Elbow, Bruner, Chomsky, Christensen, and Moffett[1] and added these to their own.

Special Offerings

Regularly ten percent of the entering class at CCNY are "second language" students: students who speak and write other languages more fluently than they do English, or whose English is markedly influenced by another tongue. These students are placed in a sequence paralleling English 1 and 2, but spreading each of these over two semesters. This English as a Second Language sequence joins the basic writing sequence in English 3. ESL courses entail drill in grammar, vocabulary, and idiom, and offer conversation sessions in addition to writing conferences. But like English 1 and English 2, ESL courses are writing courses. Original essays are complemented by dictations, summaries, and paraphrases, and writing is revised as a standard procedure.

Another ten percent or so of entering students normally win exemptions from basic writing because of demonstrated skill. They are encouraged, but not required, to take at least one writing course. Our advanced composition offerings are courses in writing for the humanities, writing for the social sciences, and technical writing, all designed to help the student to write well in his major field. We also offer creative writing courses in fiction, poetry, drama, and film and television writing.

In 1973, during the hiatus between the strictures of entry by grade-point and the strictures of tuition, the English department established a Master of Arts Program in Pedagogy to equip aspiring students to teach in programs like ours. The pedagogy program offered courses in social dialects, comparative grammars, and pedagogy, in which students read theories of writing instruction, analyzed the prose of students in the basic writing program, learned teaching strategies, and wrote syllabuses. The master's program culminated in a project researching student writing. Graduates of this program were hired as adjuncts to teach in the basic writing program. The pedagogy program has since all but succumbed to increased tuition and a tightening job market in college teaching.

Staffing

Though some SEEK composition courses were undertaken by senior professors and professional writers in the English department, most were taught by junior faculty hired for the purpose. The burst of enrollment under open admissions brought more new faculty, but also dispersed basic writing throughout the department, so numerous were the sections that had to be offered. Our basic writing courses now just outnumber the other English department offerings, and all faculty in all ranks in the department teach at least one basic writing course each semester.

In the spring of 1976, thirteen nontenured faculty were fired from the English department. Their basic writing courses were assumed by tenured faculty from departments suffering underenrollment as a result of relaxed liberal arts requirements in a time of strong career orientation among college students. Though no policy has been established regarding this irregular instruction, in the fall of 1976 twenty-four sections of basic writing were taught by faculty from the departments of history, classical languages, romance languages, and economics. Forty-five basic writing sections were allotted to outside faculty for the fall of 1977.

Notes

[1] Peter Elbow, *Writing Without Teachers* (New York: Oxford University Press, 1973); Jerome S. Bruner, *The Process of Education* (New York: Vintage, 1963); Noam Chomsky, *Aspects of the Theory of Syntax* (Cambridge, Mass.: MIT Press, 1965); Francis Christensen and Bonniejean Christensen, *A New Rhetoric* (New York: Harper & Row, 1976); James Moffett, *Teaching the Universe of Discourse* (Boston: Houghton Mifflin, 1968).

The Writing Program at Queens College of the City University of New York

Donald McQuade, Director of the Writing Program

Department responsible for the composition program   English
Full-time faculty in the department   87
Enrollment policies
    Maximum Enrollment   25 (17 for English 01)
    Minimum Enrollment   10
    Average Enrollment   23 (16 in English 01)
Staffing
    Percentage of freshman composition courses taught by graduate students   65
    Percentage taught by part-time faculty (excluding graduate students)   5
    Percentage taught by full-time instructors or lecturers   10
    Percentage taught by assistant, associate, and full professors   20
Program size
    Number of students enrolled in the freshman composition program in the fall term of 1976   2,640
    Number of sections of freshman composition offered in the fall term of 1976   120
    Number of sections at all levels—literature, composition, film, graduate, undergraduate, etc.—offered by the department in the fall term of 1976   230

The writing program at Queens College began as a piecemeal process of sorting out successful elements to add to an ever-increasing stockpile of classroom resources. These distinctly personal theories and methods—and the assumptions and data that informed them—eventually formed a constellation of intentions, a gathering of related principles and procedures for how writing could best be taught. But the open admissions program, begun at the City University of New York in the fall of 1970, soon demanded that the teaching of writing be based on more than good will and the accumulation of individual discoveries and inventions. To work effectively with so many students who were so new to higher education and whose needs were so pressing, we had to reexamine assumptions, reconstruct theories, and redesign strategies for teaching writing. Such formidable tasks rarely can be accomplished by an individual and never overnight. To trace the development of the writing program at Queens College is to describe a gradual transformation from the privacy of personal practices to a collective enterprise that opened abundant prospects for intellectual and professional growth—for students *and* faculty.

Open admissions became the locus of a shared professional commitment in the face of unprecedented circumstances. Thrust into an immensely complicated political situation, with no time to prepare paradigms for teaching basic skills to severely underprepared college students, we had little choice at first but to rely on one another. To compensate for our individual inexperience, we shared whatever knowledge we could glean about whatever worked best with each of our classes. And since we all were failing in some ways, we encouraged one another to report frustrations and disappointments. As teachers of writing, we had informally created a community of inquiry, with the expectation of some synthesis of practice and perhaps even some measure of success. That interdependence produced what we now take to be the special features of our writing program.[1]

We began by culling from innumerable student conferences and frequent conversations with secondary-school teachers and our colleagues throughout the network of CUNY colleges[2] as much reliable information as possible about our students, the nature and extent of their experiences with writing, and the attitudes they had adopted toward language. What we discovered early on in open admissions still characterizes the majority of students entering Queens College. The largest percentage enter with high-school averages well over eighty; most come from lower- and middle-class "working" families; many are first-generation college students; and nearly all of them—at least at the beginning of their composition classes—lack self-confidence and consequently are extremely passive, more spectators to than participants in educational experiences. We learned, too, that by the time they have reached the final year of secondary school they have done so little writing that they are unaccustomed to regarding it as an intellectual resource, as the natural extension of thought, and as a means of self-exploration and articulation. Given the conditions in high-school English departments (teachers conducting an average of five classes a day with thirty-five students in each), writing became an activity so alien to most students that it was an occasion to be feared. But the fact that so many young people were entering Queens College with such minimal experiences with writing eventually convinced us that it would be much more accurate and appropriate to consider them *beginning* writers rather than so-called "remedial" students. And while the popular magazines branded them as needing "bonehead" English, we concluded that what they really could use was encouragement, direction, confidence, and, perhaps most important, training in the essentials of composition, which they very well may never have had.

Over the past seven years, the English department has responded to these circumstances by developing what is now a three-semester sequence of composition courses: English 01, 1, and 6. (English 1 and 6 currently are required for graduation.) All entering students take a two-hour placement examination, consisting of an impromptu writing exercise and the English Cooperative Test, a short-answer evaluation of the students' command of grammar and vocabulary as well as their reading comprehension. The essays of those students who score above fifty on this part of the test are read by two or, if necessary, three members of the department. (All English faculty participate in evaluating placement examinations.) On the basis of this twofold assessment, students enroll in the appropriate course in the composition sequence. The design of the program and the formulation of the principles that underlie it represent the spirit and substance of the department's collaborative efforts to meet its students' needs and help them gain appreciable control over their verbal lives. And while this purpose has remained consistent over the years, the content and shape of the freshman English program have changed considerably.

The courses offered at the onset of open admissions could not respond to the apparent needs of so many students who entered the college with such a wide range in writing and reading aptitudes. In 1970, English 1 and 2—consisting of composition and an introduction to literature—stood as the remnants of what had once been a required four-semester sequence of writing and reading courses. But in the aftermath of the political and educational upheavals of the late sixties, the Academic Senate at Queens College voted, in the year open admissions began, to abolish all required courses except English 1. The English department then had to take on the burden of carrying a course that had packed into a single semester all the essential activities accumulated from what had formerly been a two-year course of study. Slowly, and with considerable distress, the English faculty trimmed the literature component to the point where they could honestly expect to teach writing—but to swelling ranks of students who barely had any practice in it. The convergence of this overloaded course with the large number of beginning writers who were unprepared to take on such an ill-defined, voluminous semester's work created an immediate need for a more gradual and clearly focused introduction to college writing. Designed to precede English 1, this basic course would be structured with a new emphasis: to familiarize students with the process, satisfaction, and discipline of composing, thereby opening them to the prospects of making writing a pleasurable activity for the rest of their lives.

"Introduction to English Composition" (English 01/3 credits) is intended for our least experienced writers, those whose prose is weakened by a high incidence of grammatical error and inadequate control of sentence structure. Such students lack confidence in their own skills and have marked problems developing three or four paragraphs of coherent prose. This course has, since its inception in 1970, formed the "philosophical" basis of our writing program. Nearly all of the distinctive traits of our composition sequence emerged during the development of English 01—and have gradually been extended into English 1 and 6, giving the program a consistent conceptual design.

English 01, like the courses that follow it, attempts to satisfy the demands of college-level writing by creating and sustaining a nonpunitive environment in which inexperienced writers compose with such frequency that they no longer consider the activity threatening. By writing often and attentively enough, students experience how writing extends thought. In addition to constant practice with such prewriting exercises as heuristics, invention, brainstorming, journal keeping, "nonstop" and focused "free-writing" (what Northrop Frye called "associative prose"), students spend a great deal of time in English 01 working with the form most congenial to them—narration. Writing short, concrete narrative essays each day about their own experiences to illustrate an abstract point or a generalization can provide considerable success immediately and help strengthen their confidence when they are asked later in the semester to create more complicated structures for their observations and ideas.

Since the course is designed to lead students deliberately through the stages of the composing process, they become accustomed to writing several drafts in order to discover their subjects, sharpen their focus, and shape the content of their essays. So too, since their own writing serves as the primary text in the course, students are anxious to have their work viewed from the perspectives of their peers and instructors. Accordingly, students work energetically and efficiently in small groups to solve common problems in writing and reading. They regularly submit working drafts to groups, expect constructive responses to their prose, and revise their essays with a much better sense of purpose, audience, occasion, and tone than they possessed at the first writing. In the process, they learn to augment their own abilities to articulate their responses to the writing of others. Throughout the semester, students attend to questions of grammar that arise in the samples of their own prose, with a special emphasis given in class discussions to the sentence and its potential.

After students have developed the confidence necessary to describe the states of consciousness they value, to draw inferences from their observations and descriptions, and to generalize and abstract from their experiences, they proceed to work with the forms of expository writing they will need to master in order to achieve marked success in their major and elective courses and to participate fully in the intellectual life of the college community. Later in the semester, they concentrate on such rhetorical forms as argumentation and analysis as final preparation for extended practice in English 1 and 6 in the standard patterns of freshman composition. Many students who enter the course predisposed to regarding their lives on paper as uninteresting and to avoiding claiming any authority for their perceptions gradually come—through constant practice—to write prolifically, fluently, and more assuredly about themselves and the world around them.

With a shared purpose and general agreement about the most effective ways to begin a basic course, teachers of writing regularly prepare—on the basis of their experience in the program—a number of speculative, admittedly tentative, yet highly deliberate and engaging syllabuses for the course. These outlines set a tone and direction for the semester's work rather than list a daily schedule of particular activities. By no means do they pretend to be prescriptions for success. And although early versions frequently turn out to be overly ambitious and require modification as the semester progresses, the syllabuses create the opportunity for more people to participate in establishing the nature and direction of this basic skills course.

All faculty teaching English 01 are asked to affiliate with a particular syllabus, an arrangement that lends a good deal of coherence and flexibility to the course. The syllabuses also provide useful guides for new teachers and involve experienced faculty more deeply in the writing program. Designed to serve as occasions for conversation, the syllabuses help focus and enrich the conversation clusters that invariably form in the crowded corridors and offices of the department at the end of each class session. So too, these course plans constitute a fertile common ground for the theoretical explorations that highlight the informal staff meetings scheduled biweekly throughout the year.

Each spring, we invite new proposals and circulate them among the staff, and, if several teachers indicate that they wish to work with a syllabus, we adopt it as an alternative for the following semester. The vast majority of writing teachers seem enthusiastic about this method of organizing the course. And the success of several faculty at seeing their syllabuses through to publication as textbooks undoubtedly helps convince other instructors that working up syllabuses is a worthwhile investment of their professional talents and energies.[3]

The department has recently adapted and extended the principle of preparing common syllabuses for basic writing by publishing a series of statements on its expectations of student writing performance. Distributed to all students at the first meeting of every writing class in the composition sequence, these statements identify precisely what is expected of every student's writing by the end of each semester's work. The expectation sheets significantly reduce students' anxieties about grades, since they always have an exact frame of reference to chart the progress of their work during the semester. So too, the expectation sheets, reprinted in the course descriptions circulated among faculty, provide a clear set of objectives for planning courses and help differentiate one course from the next in the sequence. The expectation sheets also remind students and faculty that they are participating in basic skills courses, and that skills develop in time, with practice. Such a shared attitude creates the maximum opportunity for students to do well but also imposes the responsibility that they improve their skills. Using the expectation sheets as a basis, faculty and students can collaborate to achieve these goals.

In order to create as collaborative an environment as possible in their writing classes, and to increase the number of responses to each piece of student writing, many of those scheduled to teach basic writing participate in the department's team teaching program, which matches an experienced writing instructor with an undergraduate team teacher. They share full responsibility for planning their writing course, converting their syllabus into daily exercises for inexperienced writers, and responding to a wealth of student writing. From a very modest beginning seven years ago as an experiment in a few sections, the program has grown to involve well over one half of those teaching freshman English.

Each year, the several hundred undergraduate applicants are carefully screened in a series of rigorous interviews with the faculty coordinator of the program and several members of the department who regularly participate in it. Candidates are selected for such qualities as their general intelligence, commitment to writing, ability to listen, sensitivity to the problems of inexperienced writers, and adaptability to the shifting cricumstances of classroom activities. No preference is given to English or education majors, though they certainly are not excluded. Most undergraduate team teachers work in the program for a year, and all register each semester for a four-credit course, "Writing Good Prose." They spend three hours each week team teaching a basic writing course and the fourth hour in a weekly seminar involving the other undergraduate teachers and the coordinator of the program. At these sessions, team teachers discuss strategies for teaching writing, consider the full range of practical, everyday instructional problems, and, when they have gained some experience, speculate about the more theoretical aspects of rhetoric and grammar. The undergraduate team teachers keep journals of their work in which they accumulate and develop fresh insights into the difficulties and satisfactions of less experienced writers.

The supportive environment of the writing program is augmented by the work of the Writing Skills Workshop, a free tutorial service available from 9:00 A.M. to 9:00 P.M. each day to those in the college community who wish to strengthen their writing skills. The workshop is a resource center familiar to the general student population; it is not restricted to those who have serious writing problems. Students attend voluntarily, and most work with the same tutors throughout a series of appointments. When the budget permits, "one-on-one" tutoring is conducted by trained peer tutors, graduate students, and teaching assistants funded through the federal government's Comprehensive Employment Training Act. Before the budget cuts struck CUNY, full-time lecturers from the English department, in lieu of teaching a basic writing course, also served in the workshop as supervisors and tutors, thereby providing an important link between the faculty and the tutoring staff. The director of the workshop is a member of the English department who also teaches writing each semester. The policy of the workshop staff is to treat students as writers and to regard their prose sympathetically and respectfully as literature. Tutors are able to reinforce their tutees' command of diction and syntax as well as to convey methods for thinking through ideas more logically and concisely, and with greater complexity. The workshop staff often creates its own teaching materials, both rhetorical and grammatical, contributes to the department's file of mimeographed exercises and assignments, and draws on the department's library of composition texts and professional journals devoted to writing.

The Writing Skills Workshop's peer and graduate tutors, as well as English faculty and undergraduate team teachers, are trained through a series of informal staff meetings held throughout the year. We begin with a full day of workshops in September. These sessions not only provide detailed information on the writing backgrounds of entering students but also include consideration of the aims and concerns of the program as well as discussion of the assumptions and suggested exercises in the syllabuses prepared for each course. Biweekly meetings each semester follow up on the matters introduced in September and explore additional topics proposed by those teaching in the program. These sessions tend to treat practical issues, although more recently there has been increasing interest in the theoretical aspects of rhetoric and teaching writing. The usual format calls for two instructors (preferably a graduate fellow and a full-time teacher) to make a short presentation, followed by a discussion of such topics as reading and writing as related activities, how and when to teach argumentation, increasing a student's powers of observation, effective strategies for working in small groups, and grammar in the composition class. Other meetings provide occasions for teachers to regroup with their colleagues who are following the same syllabus and exchange notes on their respective successes and failures. Each meeting is repeated on three days for the convenience of the staff, with a different pair of discussion leaders scheduled for each session.

The English department extended the collaborative spirit of these composition staff meetings when its faculty began to work with colleagues in other departments to reinforce the basic writing skills our students had developed in freshman composition through continued practice in the elective courses of their major fields of study. Working in less pressured circumstances than those for English 01, the department set out to involve the entire college community in improving writing across the curriculum by making it a significant activity throughout a student's academic career. At the same time, the dramatic enrollment increases in the English department's intermediate and advanced expository writing courses indicated that many students want or need continued training in writing. Accordingly, the Academic Senate voted in the spring of 1976 to require a second semester of composition for graduation.

To provide the strongest motivation and usefulness for such additional work in composition, the English department established, in addition to general expository writing sections, special sections designed to increase students' writing competence in their fields of concentration. Students majoring in biology, chemistry, or physics, for example, may now take a course in "Writing about the Natural Sciences"; those majoring in fields such as sociology, anthropology, or psychology may register for "Writing about the Social Sciences." Those special sections include:

English 6.0	General Expository Writing
6.1	Writing about Business and Economics
6.2	Writing about the Law
6.3	Writing about the Natural Sciences
6.4	Writing for Pre-Med Students
6.5	Writing for Prospective Teachers
6.6	Writing about the Social Sciences
6.7	Writing about Literature
6.8	Writing about Music
6.9	Writing about Art

The department began with a modest number of such offerings, but student interest prompted an increase, albeit cautious, in the number of such popular sections as "Writing about the Law" and "Writing about Business and Economics." So too, when enrollment warranted, the department has scheduled even more specific sections—for example, "Writing about the Computer Sciences." If the demand is sufficient, all students, whatever their major, may eventually have a specialized course made available to them.

Where suitable texts for these courses exist—see, for example, the recent spate of textbooks on business writing—these constitute, in addition to the students' own writing, the basic materials for the course. Where they are not available, teachers assemble, with the welcomed assistance of faculty in other departments, appropriate materials from professional journals. Insofar as possible, training and exercises are geared to the students' professional aims.

Students are urged to enroll in these courses as soon as they have completed English 1. And since most students take them when they have just launched their major, their instructors are competent to guide them even if they themselves have no more than a sound, general grounding in the discipline they are training their students to write for. After all, the fundamental operations in any writing course are obviously applicable to any discipline.

The results of the English department's survey of the professional backgrounds, interests, and resources of its personnel established that a sizable percentage of its faculty had, or could readily attain, the requisite degree of competence to teach one or other of these special courses. But only those members who consented were scheduled to teach them. That number has increased steadily each semester. More writing teachers are now able to respond to the writing needs and interests of more students as well as to support the work of colleagues in other departments.

From working with inexperienced and insecure writers in English 01 to help them gain appreciable writing proficiency to joining with other departments to sustain our students' mastery of fundamental skills, teachers in the writing program at Queens College endeavor to create a collaborative environment in which their students will no longer regard writing as a subject in competition with their other courses. In each of the three courses in the writing sequence, students are encouraged to recognize writing as a process that unifies all of the disparate experiences of their verbal lives. And with the aid of continued practice, they can discover the benefits of making writing an accustomed extension of their thinking. Writing becomes, then, an opportunity for students to train themselves to make distinctions, an activity fundamental to learning, and one that is applicable to any of their major interests. No doubt this is a challenging and, at times, frustrating task for English departments, but it is an essential one, not only if they aim to teach students to write well and to make writing a pleasant and enduring enterprise but also if they expect their students to understand, evaluate, and participate fully and successfully in the events and culture of a modern democracy.

Notes

[1] For a full consideration of the possible applications of the principles of collaborative learning to developing writing programs, see M. L. J. Abercrombie, *The Anatomy of Judgment* (London, 1960; rpt. New York: Basic Books, 1962); A. K. C. Ottaway, *Learning*

through Group Experiences (New York: Humanities Press, 1966); Edwin Mason, *Collaborative Learning* (New York: 1972; rpt. New York: Schocken, 1973); Kenneth Brufee, *A Short Course in Writing* (Cambridge, Mass.: Winthrop, 1972); Kenneth Brufee, "Collaborative Learning: Some Practical Models," *College English*, 34 (1973), 634–43; Ronnie Dugger, "Cooperative Learning in a Writing Community," *Change*, 8 (1976), 30–33; Thom Hawkins, *Group Inquiry Techniques for Teaching Writing* (Urbana: NCTE, 1976).

For an excellent guide to teaching basic writing, see Mina P. Shaugnessy, *Errors and Expectations* (New York: Oxford, 1977).

[2] These early conversations with secondary-school teachers led to the formation in 1972 of Common Concerns of English Educators, an informal alliance of chairpersons in English in the secondary schools of Queens County and their counterparts in the CUNY colleges of that borough. This group continues to meet to exchange significant information and to consider issues relevant to student writing skills at both levels. For a discussion of the possibilities of collaborating with high-school teachers of English, see my essay, " 'Who Do You Think You're Talking To?': Trading Ideas for Insults in the English Profession," *English Journal*, 65 (1976), 8–10.

In 1973, the faculty charged with directing writing programs within the City University established CAWS, the CUNY Association of Writing Supervisors, to disseminate information about writing programs and effective teaching strategies, coordinate curricula, set up study groups on the theoretical aspects of writing, and initiate research projects.

[3] Among the textbooks developed from syllabuses used at Queens College are Robert Atwan and Donald McQuade, *Popular Writing in America* (New York: Oxford, 1974); David Herrstrom, Elizabeth Morgan, and Ron Morgan, *Writing as Discovery* (Cambridge, Mass.: Winthrop, 1976); Robert Lyons, *Autobiography: A Reader for Writers* (New York: Oxford, 1977); Sandra Schor and Judith Fishman, *The Random House Guide to Basic Writing* (New York: Random House, 1978).

The First-Year Writing Program at the University of Virginia

Charlene M. Sedgwick, Director of
the First-Year Writing Program

Department responsible for the writing program   English
Full-time faculty in the department   52
Enrollment policies
>   Maximum Enrollment   18
>   Minimum Enrollment   8
>   Average Enrollment   15

Staffing
>   Percentage of first-year writing courses taught by graduate students   96
>   Percentage taught by full-time instructors or lecturers   1
>   Percentage taught by assistant, associate, and full professors   3

Program size
>   Number of students enrolled in the first-year writing program in the fall
>   term of 1976   700
>   Number of sections of first-year writing offered in the fall term of 1976   44
>   Number of sections at all levels—literature, composition, film, graduate,
>   undergraduate, etc.—offered by the department in the fall term of
>   1976   211

Twenty years ago students at the University of Virginia had to take two semesters of expository writing, one half of a two-year English requirement. All of the composition sections, numbering fifteen students each, were taught by full-time members of the English department, who assigned a standard text (Gorrell and Laird's *Modern English Handbook*) and a grammar workbook with tear-out worksheets. Although there was advanced placement for skilled writers, no student was entirely exempted from the composition requirement. This format, thought by some to represent the Golden Age of Freshman Composition, began to change in the early sixties. Expanding undergraduate enrollment, the development of a full-scale graduate program, and the deployment of assistant professors in graduate courses forced the department to look elsewhere for writing teachers, and for a period of time instructors who had completed all their doctoral work but the dissertation were hired for three-year periods from other institutions. As the English department began to produce its own qualified graduate students in ever-greater numbers, it no longer had to go so far afield to man the sections of the first-year composition course. This shift in personnel from permanent, full-time faculty to graduate instructors who would teach in the program for only a few semesters coincided with the more dramatic and well-publicized curriculum changes of the late sixties and early seventies. The department had now to cope not only with the adjustments forced upon it by the rather abrupt shift from undergraduate to graduate education in the post-Sputnik era but also with changing ideas about the philosophy of teaching composition and the relaxation of undergraduate requirements. The expository writing requirement in the College of Arts and Sciences was reduced, in 1970, from two semesters to one, and roughly a third of the students in every entering class have since been exempted from any writing requirement at all on the basis of their scores on the English Achievement Test. The increase in the size of the entering class (from about 400 students in 1957 to more than 2,000 in 1977) has meant that, despite a reduction by half in the requirement and an increase by a third in advanced placement, the number of composition sections has steadily risen. Almost all of these sections are now taught by graduate instructors drawn from our doctoral program. The instructors must follow certain departmental guidelines defining the aims of the course and the responsibilities of students and teachers, but they are free to choose their own texts and to create their own syllabuses. Although the number of students in the college has risen in twenty years from 1,561 to 7,113, there are still only fifteen students registered in each expository writing section. This ideal teacher-pupil ratio is probably the one constant that has enabled us to weather the many changes of the past decade without too much stress. As I write, the university is about to implement a curriculum change restoring the second semester of the writing requirement and eliminating the policy of total exemption for some students.

This does not mean, however, that we have come full circle. We are now on the far side of the sixties, and we have a larger and more diverse undergraduate enrollment than we had twenty years ago, along with a corps of able graduate students who need teaching experience. Assessing the writing needs of our undergraduates and training the graduate instructors to teach them are our immediate concerns, and in addressing these two concerns, we are naturally forced to consider the time-honored questions: What is good style, how can it be evaluated, and how can it be taught? What does the faculty of the University of Virginia, which has charged the English department with the task of training its undergraduates to write acceptable prose, actually consider good style? The difficulty of answering these questions does not relieve us of the responsibility to do so. The turnover of teaching personnel in the first-year writing course and the relatively short time our students spend in a composition class force us to define our principles clearly and to adhere to a few simple and practical goals that will make sense to both teachers and students. Chief among those principles we stress is the principle of "readability." Charged by the faculty to teach incoming students to write acceptable (i.e., readable) examinations, lab reports, and term papers in a number of academic disciplines, our instructors must define readability in comparative rather than absolute terms. Prose is more readable when the reader needs less time and effort to understand its meaning securely. Thus the reader's time and effort must be accommodated to the concepts and attitudes that are being conveyed. This does not mean that we teach our students to communicate their ideas by oversimplifying them. Rather, the challenge is to enable them to express their most complex ideas and values in simple form. In order to do this, they must be made aware, first, of the peculiarity of prose writing that results from the absence of social context and, second, of the psychological bases of readability that make it necessary for the writer to establish expectations in the reader and to fulfill these expectations as soon as possible.

Because most of our students have never been obliged to consider the effect that the absence of an audience has upon their ability to communicate, we teach them as soon as possible to recognize how much of the potential for ambiguity is removed by the immediate context of oral speech. Compared to normal conversation, writing carries very little orienting context at all; therefore, it must create its own context and must secure meaning by techniques that have evolved over several centuries in all written languages. We tell our students to orient their reader to a subject and attitude as early as possible and, in some form or other, to fulfill the expectations thus raised. To do this they must consider the psychological principles that govern the reader's comprehension of a text. Indeed, there are so many ways of crafting readable sentences and paragraphs that the statement of a few of these psychological principles has served us better than the numerous and arbitrary maxims that clutter the textbooks. Parallel constructions and expectation markers like "on the other hand," "neither . . . nor," "similarly," and so forth, give the reader some sense of the direction a sentence or paragraph will take. The form in which information is conveyed should enable the reader to grasp its content with ease. To communicate "information" about thought and attitude, however, the writer must deviate slightly from the absolutely predictable and fulfill expectations in a slightly unexpected way. Clichés and formulaic expressions, which are highly readable, convey very little meaning. Thus we try to teach our students to cope with the often conflicting demands that result from the psychology of the reader. The reader must not stumble or go astray for want of syntactic predictors and a frame of reference, but at the same time the writer's style must not be so predictable or fomulaic that the reader loses interest and fails, through inattention, to get the point. We make our students examine their own reactions as readers by asking them to criticize each other's essays in class. In order to develop criteria for criticizing each other's writing, they must identify the stylistic and syntactic devices that aid comprehension and sustain interest; they must recognize how, in less successful efforts, the lack of such devices will lead to confusion and inattention. Every composition section is a workshop in which the student's role as a member of the audience is as important as his role as a writer. Our students are taught to ask routinely what expectations a writer has created, and whether, or how, these expectations have been fulfilled.

Expectations must not only be created and fulfilled; they must be fulfilled as quickly as possible. On the sentence level, this doctrine is closely related to Strunk's maxims "Keep related words together" and "Omit needless words."[1] Both are ways of fulfilling expectations and removing uncertainties. Rapid closure is one of the main principles we ask our students to consider when rewriting their own work. It helps them recognize how far the reader can stray before reaching the end even of a sentence, and instills in them the habit of preventing unexpected excursions. Thus, what we are teaching our students is not clarity and logic of thought, the acquisition of which desirable traits is the goal of most of their college courses. We are teaching principles of revision for attaining readability. The course could in fact be called "principles of revision," since the editorial revising process is essential to composition even when it is a mental process for practiced writers engaged in their first draft.[2]

With these principles and goals in mind, we try, then, to strike a balance in the classroom between the uniformity necessary to achieve a fair evaluation of students registered in a multisectioned course and the freedom necessary to enable our instructors to teach in a manner best suited to their own temperaments and interests. Thus, although we limit the number of pages a student in the course must read to two hundred, instructors are allowed to choose their own texts. We do recommend the use of a concise handbook, such as Strunk and White's *Elements of Style*, or Thomas Pinney's *Short Handbook and Style Sheet*, but our instructors are free to teach without using a text if they so wish. A great many do assign a reader, such as Kane and Peters' *Writing Prose*, to provide subject matter for essays, and some use short stories or poems—keeping in mind, however, that they are not teaching a literature course. In the same way, instructors choose their own topics for assignments, limited only by the departmental regulation that every student must write one essay a week of about five hundred words. A questionnaire, which is really a student evaluation form, is distributed to instructors before they teach and filled out by students at the end of the semester. The evaluation form helps to remind instructors of departmental guidelines, because the questions, which were made up by the instructors themselves, point to the general goals of the course. We have used this evaluation for six semesters and believe that it has accomplished its purpose. Not only has it kept instructors within departmental guidelines; it has also been a useful pedagogical device. The students' remarks, which are usually fair, thoughtful, and constructive, give us the kind of information we need to improve our teaching.

We recommend to our instructors that they turn the course into a writing workshop centered around the reading and criticism of the students' own essays. Attendance is compulsory, and the students are graded for their contributions to class discussion as well as for their writing. The reading aloud in class of student writing we have found to be an extremely effective technique for teaching composition, for there is a direct correlation between the actual readability of an essay and the listener's comprehension when it is read aloud. The more readable the prose, the easier it is for the audience to understand the essay the first time around. When reading silently, a person can backtrack and linger over a passage until he finally deciphers it, and even the most opaque prose will finally yield some meaning under intense scrutiny. Reading aloud, however, forces the writer to be explicit, provide adequate transitions, and employ whatever stylistic and syntactic devices the reader needs to follow his train of thought. Reading aloud also provides a real audience for the author and enables the teacher to escape the role of lone critic and authority figure. After an essay has been read aloud, the instructor asks questions related to the author's intentions and the success with which those intentions have been fulfilled, using the blackboard and in-class writing to explore the possible solutions to a particular writing problem. Whole essays, or parts of them, such as first or last paragraphs, and even groups of sentences, are reproduced and distributed to the class for comments. In the course of the semester, the students' own essays usually bring to light most of the topics that are dealt with more systematically in the textbooks.

The difficult and time-consuming task of writing constructive comments on the students' weekly essays and the problem of judging these essays in absolute terms (i.e., assigning a grade) are at the heart of any composition course. The nature of this problem of evaluation and the extreme differences of opinion on the subject that arise among even the most experienced writing teachers have been well documented[3] and are painfully familiar to anyone who has taught composition or participated in a joint grading session. We must, in all honesty, face up to these differences among ourselves and recognize the extent to which our particular tastes, idiosyncrasies, and personal responses to given students affect our ability to evaluate their writing fairly. In order to check these subjective tendencies, those of us who teach composition engage in a series of exercises designed to explore the various means of criticizing student essays and to regularize our system of evaluation. A set of about four or five student essays is first distributed to ten instructors, who meet together to comment on them and rank and grade them. These individuals then become the leaders of other small workshops of instructors where the process is repeated. All the instructors must rank and grade the essays and read their comments aloud to the group. This procedure invariably generates a lively, and often heated, exchange among the instructors and usually leads directly to broad discussions of criteria for judging writing and of pedagogical strategies. Not only have the workshops eliminated at least some of the disparities in our evaluation of the students' writing; they have also enabled us to share our ideas and concerns and to seek our colleagues' advice. Although it is often nerve-wracking and painful to expose one's judgments, we think the workshops are worth the effort. Our training program for new instructors consists of two days of these sessions at the beginning of their first semester of teaching; in addition, for two days during *each* semester the entire composition faculty participates in such workshops. All instructors also participate in a cross-grading exercise every semester in which they pair off, assign the same topic to their classes, exchange papers for grading and comments, and then meet to settle their differences.

At the first class meeting of each semester a take-home diagnostic assignment is prepared by the department and given to every student registered in the course. It consists of a seven-hundred word essay, and its purpose is two-fold: it enables instructors to exempt from the course students who write well, even though they did not score 660 on the English Achievement Test, and, more important, it gives the instructor, as soon as possible, some notion of the general writing ability of a particular class. If a student's work for the semester is graded lower than a *C*, he receives a *No Credit* (which is not computed in his grade point average) and must repeat the course until he passes it. For several years we have operated a writing center where students with severe writing problems can work with tutors for as long as they wish. The center, staffed by graduate students with some teaching experience, serves not only the incoming students but all undergraduate and graduate students as well. Students volunteer for tutoring, and there is no credit attached to their work in the writing center.

At the end of the semester, every instructor submits to the department a "retrospective syllabus," an informal report of the semester's work. It includes the topics for weekly assignments, a discussion of texts used, a description of in-class writing exercises, and general comments on the success or failure of various assignments and teaching strategies. We make these syllabuses available to all the instructors; newly appointed instructors, who sometimes have trouble envisioning what actually goes on in a composition class, have found them especially useful. Another aid to new instructors is a handbook that includes a discussion of those principles set forth at the beginning of this article, a description of the grading sessions, some suggestions for teaching the course, administrative details, and documents relating to the course, such as the student evaluation form, a sample diagnostic essay, and a "cover sheet" for weekly assignments designed to help students plan their essays.

There are many problems connected with the course that we have yet to solve. Although the grading sessions have eliminated some of the inequities in our evaluation of the students' writing, we are still very far from being truly objective, if objectivity is indeed possible. The effect that the choice of a particular topic has upon the quality of a student's writing is difficult to determine, as is the effect of the compulsory nature of the course. Are we doing enough for our students whose high-school preparation was weak, and do we need to establish special remedial sections? Should the course be diversified, with certain sections concentrating on special writing genres such as "technical writing"? Should credit be attached to the work a student does in the writing center? What effect does grading have upon the students' efforts? The list could go on, and none of the items enumerated would surprise anyone engaged in teaching composition. More research into some of these questions is obviously needed, and those of us who formulate and administer writing programs must be open-minded and willing to institute change where there is a need for change. That faculty interest in student writing has begun to revive at the University of Virginia is encouraging. One sign of this revival is the broadening of the undergraduate writing requirement. It is not yet clear how the responsibility for the new requirement will be divided among the English department and other departments in the university, but one thing is certain: the formula of clearly stated principles combined with a flexible approach to the actual teaching of the expository writing course has already served us well. It helps to keep the instructors on the same theoretical track, while at the same time enabling them to respond with some spontaneity and imagination to the immediate and constantly changing needs of their students.

Notes

1 William Strunk, Jr., and E. B. White, *The Elements of Style* (New York: Macmillan, 1962), p. 17.

2 The teaching goals that I have outlined are set forth in a "White Paper" by E. D. Hirsch, Jr.—our director of composition in recent years. His essay forms part of a booklet, *ENWR 101 Instructors' Handbook*, given to every new teacher of the course.

3 Paul B. Diederich, *Measuring Growth in English* (Urbana, Ill.: NCTE, 1974).

The Composition Program at J. Sargeant Reynolds Community College, Parham Campus

Lawrence N. Kasden, Chairman of the English Department

Department responsible for the composition program   Humanities and Social Sciences

Full-time faculty in English   11

Enrollment policies
    Maximum Enrollment   25
    Minimum Enrollment   10
    Average Enrollment   21

Staffing
    Percentage of freshman composition courses taught by part-time faculty   30
    Percentage taught by full-time instructors or lecturers   21
    Percentage taught by assistant, associate, and/or full professors   49

Program size
    Number of students enrolled in the freshman composition program in the fall term of 1976   1,063
    Number of sections of freshman composition offered in the fall term of 1976   42
    Number of sections at all levels—literature, composition, film, etc.—offered by the department in the fall term of 1976   75

The Parham Campus of J. Sargeant Reynolds Community College began offering classes at a temporary location in 1973. The following year the permanent campus structure was opened, and the college opened a second campus in a temporary facility. In addition to offering courses at these two locations, each campus schedules classes at rented facilities, correctional institutions, and community centers. In total, the college has offered classes at some sixty-five locations. Because there are some differences among the English programs offered at the various locations, primarily in the areas of basic studies and electives, I will confine my remarks to the Parham Campus.

The college serves three somewhat overlapping clienteles: college transfer students, those who will later transfer to four-year institutions to earn bachelor's degrees; vocational students, those who are earning two-year terminal degrees and one-year certificates; and "walk-in" students, those who wish to increase their knowledge or upgrade their skills but do not seek a degree or certificate. For the first group the college offers a traditional English composition sequence that may be followed by elective courses. For the two-year program students and many of the certificate students, the college offers a two-quarter sequence entitled "Communications Skills." In general, this sequence includes grammar review, business writing, library research, and, for engineering students, technical writing. Additional composition electives and required courses are offered for students in certain special programs. Walk-in students may, of course, take any of the composition courses. In addition to offering composition courses, the department offers creative writing, journalism, literature, and what can only be termed a wide selection of odds and ends.

Because the college has an open-door admissions policy, many students are not prepared to take either of the composition sequences or to take the other courses mentioned. For these students—and their number is substantial—the department offers basic skills courses in reading, writing, and English as a Second Language. Since these courses, and their counterparts in math, reflect the community college's unique role of providing the chance for continued education for all in the Richmond metropolitan area who desire it, the basic skills courses are considered by many people to be the most important ones offered by the English department. This attitude is partially demonstrated by the fact that most of these courses are taught by full-time faculty, and that most of the full-time faculty regularly teach at least one such course each quarter.

Before describing in more detail the various writing courses and the testing program used for placement, I will make a few comments about the faculty. The department consists of the equivalent of sixteen full-time members, of whom eleven are in fact full-time. All part-time and full-time faculty have at least the master's degree. Of the eleven full-time faculty, three have Ph.D.'s, one is an A.B.D., two have double master's degrees, and three others have done substantial work beyond the M.A. Besides degrees in English and English education, the faculty members have degrees or extensive backgrounds in reading, English as a Second Language, journalism, and creative writing. In addition, the specializations of the faculty cover each of the traditional areas of English and American literatures and popular literature. I make specific mention of the faculty and their credentials because careful attention was paid in choosing persons who could enable the small department to offer a wide variety of programs. Whenever necessary, if additional staffing is needed in a specialized area, the faculty member specially trained in that area conducts either formal or informal in-service training for his colleagues.

Testing

All students are given placement tests in writing and reading, and nonnative speakers are required to take an English proficiency test. Whenever possible, the tests are administered before the students enroll. In the vast majority of cases, however, the students have been tested during the first meetings of the first composition courses and in the first meetings of the basic skills courses. This has been unfortunate since valuable class time is used up and many students must add/drop into different courses as a result of their test scores. Beginning in 1977 all new students were tested before they enrolled for classes and were required to pass the writing test before entering one of the composition sequences.

For purposes of placing nonnative speakers, the department administers the University of Michigan English Placement Test and a college testing package consisting of a composition and an oral interview. On the basis of the score on these tests, a nonnative speaker is placed in a regular composition course, basic skills writing, or one of the various levels of English as a Second Language. The testing package is used because, unlike the TOEFL test, it assesses the student's ability to produce spoken and written English. A drawback to this test is that it should be administered by someone experienced in ESL.

For reading placement the department uses the McGraw-Hill Reading Placement Test, Part III, which measures comprehension and takes forty minutes to administer. The test is multiple choice and can be easily and quickly hand scored. Students who are below the fortieth percentile of the national norm for community college students are *advised* to take developmental reading. The department will probably soon assess the need to make passing the reading test a requirement for entrance into the regular composition sequences.

The writing placement test was designed by members of the department and has three parts: grammar and usage, sentence writing, and paragraph writing. A student *must* pass each section of the test in order to begin one of the composition sequences. The following exercises are part of the placement test:

Section One: Recognition

Directions: The italicized words in the sentences below are not standard for formal English. In the space provided, write the formal, standard ("correct") form.

_____ 1. I *be* playing guitar for the past ten years.
_____ 2. I *file* my tax form by March 20th, but now the Internal Revenue Service claims I was late.

—————— 3. Last year I was *work* in a factory.
—————— 4. They *does* what they please.
—————— 5. Vera and Claudette *buys* new clothes almost every week.
—————— 6. George said *they* went to the fair by himself.
—————— 7. Spike and *him* go bowling every Friday night.
—————— 8. *Charlie* book was found in the road.
—————— 9. *Hold* their breath, they jumped into the river.
——————10. She *exercise* for twenty minutes every day.

Section Two: Sentence Combining

Directions: The groups of sentences below can be combined in various ways into just one sentence per group. In the space provided combine the sentences in each group into one sentence per group.

Example: 1. The present moment is electric.
2. The present moment sparks with life.
3. The present moment crackles with possibilities.
4. The possibilities are untried.
The present moment is electric, sparking with life, and crackling with untried possibilities. (This sentence is one way among many to combine the four above. *A few words may change, but no important idea should be left out.*)

Group A: 1. The groom stands in a room.
2. The room is off to the side.
3. The room is in the church.
4. He waits anxiously.
5. He tries to smile.

Group B: 1. The go-go dancer stared at the window.
2. The go-go dancer was bird-faced.
3. The go-go dancer was thin.
4. The window was rain-smeared.
5. The go-go dancer watched the rain.
6. The go-go dancer thought about her boy friend.
7. The boy friend was in the front row.

Section Three: Short Essay

Directions: Choose *one* of the topics listed below and write a short essay—two or three paragraphs—about it on this sheet. Length: about 200 words.

Topics: 1. Explain your main reasons for coming to college.
2. Explain your main reasons for choosing the curriculum (degree or certificate program) you are entering.
3. Describe the main features of the job you hope to get after college.
4. Explain the importance of having a hobby.

The test has recently been revised so that students must actually locate un-
identified errors in usage and grammar and rewrite the sentences in which they
appear, and must write healthy paragraphs. Both the original and the revised
tests are scored in the same manner. More than two wrong on Part I is failing;
the other parts are graded holistically.

In order to ensure consistent grading by the faculty with respect to both
the placement test and course assignments, the department conducts periodic
workshops for full-time faculty, at which grading criteria are discussed and
sample themes and placement tests are graded collectively and individually.
Results are again shared and discussed, and holistic standards are agreed
upon. At this same workshop, different faculty members lead discussions on
each of the various courses in order to allow a sharing of assignments, lesson
plans, and methodology. In addition, basic course requirements are set: for
example, a minimum of six themes and a term paper should normally be
required for English 111. Most of the full-time faculty also attend similar
workshops that are held for part-time teachers. Part-time faculty are required to attend at least one such workshop per year.

Courses

At the heart of the composition program is the basic skills course—"Developmental Studies," English 01. This course carries five credits that are not
applicable for graduation but do serve for pupposes of financial aid, veterans'
benefits, and tuition charges. Students receive grades of *S* (satisfactory), *R*
(re-enroll), and *U* (unsatisfactory); and the course can be repeated for credit
as many times as necessary for the student to attain the writing skills necessary for entrance into English 101 or 111.

In the past the 01 classes have met five hours per week: three hours with
the instructor and two hours of unsupervised time in the learning resources
area of the library. Because the students have not conscientiously attended the
meetings in the library, instructors have begun meeting the class all five
hours.

On the basis of performance on the three-part placement test, the 01
student is required to complete certain materials that correspond to one or
more of the three units covered by the test. Students who fail Part I of the test
are required to work in *Keys to American English (Keys)*; students who fail
Part II work in *Sentence Combining*; and students who fail Part III work in
Paragraph Practice.[1] The fairly large number of 01 students who fail all three
parts of the test begin their work in *Keys* and progress to *Sentence Combining*
and then to *Paragraph Practice*. The other students, those who do not fail all
three parts, tend to fall into two groups: those who fail only Part I and those
who fail both Parts II and III. A student who fails more than one part of the
test will probably need at least two quarters to complete his course requirements.

Since Part I of the developmental writing course deals with standard
usage, it is understandable that most of the students who fail this unit are
from environments in which standard American dialect (grammar, inventory,
or whatever is currently the popular term) is not spoken. The textbook these

students work with provides systematic drills in the use of verbs, nouns, pronouns, and other parts of speech. Our students are required to complete the twenty-five lessons on verbs and are then pretested to determine which additional lessons they should complete. The verb section includes lessons on present and past tenses of regular verbs, *to be* present and past, *to do* present and past, and so forth through other irregular verbs in present and past; past and present perfect tenses; conditional; modals; and passive voice. Almost all of the lessons consist of a brief and clear explanation of the differences between the standard and nonstandard contructions and the same three types of drills; and consequently the students can easily progress from lesson to lesson without much assistance from the instructor. Each lesson consists of approximately 170 drill items. After students finish each lesson, they check their answers against an answer key. As they progress through the lessons, they are periodically tested to ensure that they are mastering the material.

Students in the second unit of the course work in *Sentence Combining*, a text that consists of some two hundred pages of very short stories or essays written in groups of simple sentences. The student must combine the sentences in each group into one sentence. As he works through the text, he is required to use more and more sophisticated methods of subordination and coordination. Two examples from different sections of the text show the course of development the student follows:

1. French fries are loaded into a basket.
2. The French fries are white.
3. The basket is wire.

But
1. Many of Sutton's poems are dead.
2. His lines are buried in geography.
3. His words are muffled in cliché.
4. This poem is alive.
5. This poem engages the reader.
6. This poem forces the reader to listen.
7. This poem demands a response.[2]

In the third unit of the course the student is required to write both guided paragraphs and freely written paragraphs. As the student progresses, the topics become more sophisticated, although emphasis is placed on good paragraph development and not on subject matter.

Finally, all students are required to complete for homework *English 2600*,[3] a programed grammar text. This provides them with a general understanding of such things as punctuation, parts of speech, and subordination and coordination; it also gives the students enough grammar vocabulary to make it easy for them to converse with their teachers about writing.

After the end of each class period, students in Parts II and III turn in their work to the instructor, who makes corrections and comments on the papers and returns them at the next class meeting. The only work the instructor must correct for students in Part I is the periodic mastery tests. Consequently, although the students are constantly writing during each class period, the amount of material that must be corrected is kept to a minimum. During the class periods, the instructor is free to move from student to student, helping each with individual problems as they arise. Ideally, in a class of fifteen students, the instructor should be able to work with each student individually during each class period. Even more significant, each student can work at his own pace and skip over material he already knows. These are especially important features in our case because the skills and learning abilities of our students vary greatly and because many students enroll in the class late in the quarter.

Students who complete 01 or who do not need to take it may enroll in one of the regular composition sequences. The sequence for two-year terminal degree students begins with 101, a course that is now being revised. At present the course consists of a general grammar review, sentence and paragraph writing, and the writing of a letter of application and résumé. Most of the students who take 101 progress to 102, which is also being revised. At present, this course consists of further letter writing, business correspondences, short report writing, and library use.

Students in two-year engineering programs take English 137 in place of 102. The 137 course works rather successfully and consists of library and research methods, letter writing, technical definitions, analysis and description of mechanisms, instructions, and formal report writing.

Finally, students majoring in corrections are required to take a course entitled "Writing for Corrections Majors." The course was designed by the English department at the request of the corrections department and its professional advisory board. Students in this course write various types of reports, personality profiles, and evaluation and recommendation letters.

Students in the college-transfer programs take English 111, 112, and 113. The first course consists of paragraph and theme writing, library and research methods, and the term paper. English 112 consists of writing themes about or related to short stories and to a novel. English 113 consists of writing themes about or related to drama and poetry. The term paper is required in English 111, rather than more logically in one of the later courses, because students need this instruction in order to write term papers in other courses. Faculty outside the English department have loosely agreed not to require term papers in first-quarter courses, in order to allow the students one quarter of instruction in composition and term-paper writing. Finally, students in the college-transfer engineering program are also required to take English 210, a course that consists of technical-report writing assignments similar to those in English 137, and oral presentation of the technical reports.

In an attempt to meet the full instructional needs of all members of the community, the department is designing two new and fairly unconventional programs that hold exciting promise. The first is an elective—and I emphasize the term *elective*—course in the use of standard spoken American English dialect. As it is now planned, this course will carry three credits and meet three hours per week; it will consist of oral discrimination and pattern practice drills and role-playing activities. The goal of the course is to provide instruction for those students who feel that their social or professional growth may be limited in some ways because of their use of nonstandard constructions in speech and writing. Students who are interested in the course will be carefully screened by counselors and teaching faculty to ensure that they understand the goals and nature of the course and that they wish to take it.

The second new program is one designed to meet the career needs of currently employed management personnel from the surrounding area. The department is designing one-credit writing modules in business correspondence and report writing that can be taught in one- or two-week periods at local businesses and corporations. After contractual arrangements are made between the college and the client organization, the instructor will collect copies of actual reports and letters written by the prospective students. With these he will tailor-design a writing program before the first class meeting. Thus far the department has offered one very successful class for one of Virginia's largest companies.

In brief, then, one can summarize the English composition program at the Parham Campus of J. Sargeant Reynolds Community College as a flexible one that tries to meet the writing and language needs of all the varied groups that make up the metropolitan population, while at the same time providing the type of writing instruction that is traditionally given to college students. This flexibility has increased the student-hours generated, allowing the department to hire new faculty and consequently to bring to the college people with different areas of expertise. For the community, this flexibility means that a fairly small department can offer instruction in many areas, instruction that is often offered by no other institution in the metropolitan area, and in some cases, by no other institution in the state of Virginia.

Notes

[1] Constance Gefvert et al. *Keys to American English* (New York: Harcourt Brace Jovanovich, 1975); William Strong, *Sentence Combining* (New York: Random House, 1973); Kathleen Sullivan, *Paragraph Practice* (New York: Macmillan, 1967).

[2] Strong, pp. 10, 176.

[3] Joseph Blumenthal, *English 2600* (New York: Harcourt Brace Jovanovich, 1972).

The Freshman Composition Program at the University of Texas at Austin

James L. Kinneavy, Director of Freshman Composition

Department responsible for the composition program English
Full-time faculty in the department 99
Enrollment policies
    Maximum Enrollment 25
    Minimum Enrollment 10
    Average Enrollment 24
Staffing
    Percentage of freshman composition courses taught by graduate students 69+
    Percentage taught by part-time faculty (excluding graduate students) 4+
    Percentage taught by full-time instructors or lecturers 12+
    Percentage taught by assistant, associate, and full professors 12+
Program size
    Number of students enrolled in the freshman composition program in the fall term of 1976 5,158
    Number of sections of freshman composition offered in the fall term of 1976 205
    Number of sections at all levels—literature, composition, film, graduate, undergraduate, etc.—offered by the department in the fall term of 1976 446

At the University of Texas at Austin, entering students are placed in one of three categories for their first course in freshman composition. Students who score between 550 and 620 on the English Composition Test of the CEEB are given a *B* for the first course in the freshman sequence, E 306 (see Figure 1), and go into classes designated *special* (see lower half of Figure 1); students scoring 620 or higher are given an *A* and go into the same classes. About thirty percent of entering students exempt the first course. Native students scoring below 550 on the ECT go into one of the three variants of E 306 (the choice is up to the student).

Foreign students scoring below 500 on the TOEFL test are put into one of the six levels of intensive English courses run by the International Office of the university (noncredit). Those scoring 500 or higher are placed in E 306Q.

The average student in the freshman classes is from a middle- or upper-class urban background, has an average national score on the SAT and ECT tests, and has a reading level of about twelfth grade. Only about 1.5% of these students are black, and about five percent are Chicano (this compares to a state population average of 8% and 16% respectively).

Structure of the Program and Description of the Courses

Figure 1 shows the general structure of the freshman composition courses at the university. The following descriptions of courses follow the structure of the diagram.

The intensive English courses are not properly a part of the freshman composition program. The courses are noncredit and emphasize speaking more than they emphasize writing. They are usually taught by teaching assistants from the Foreign Language Education Center.

The first course in the regular freshman writing sequence is E 306. This is a writing course with four major ingredients: a requirement of nine complete compositions between seven hundred and a thousand words in length, a rhetorical basis determining the kinds of compositions, a required handbook to integrate mechanics with the rhetorical progress of the course, and an anthologized reader illustrating and sometimes modeling the rhetorical kinds of composition. The themes embody the following rhetorical skills: classifying and defining, self-expressing, persuading, informing (library research), exploring, proving by induction, proving by deduction, explaining, and analyzing cause and effect. The *self-expressing* theme is usually accomplished by means of a journal that is kept throughout the semester and is akin to the freewriting recommended by Ken Macrorie, Peter Elbow, and Lou Kelly, among others. The *informing* paper is often combined with the exploring, explaining, and cause and effect themes to provide three small library exercises rather than one major paper isolated from the rhetorical skills.

There are three variants of the main E 306 track: E 306 for Mexican-Americans, E 306, "Individualized Instruction," and E 306Q for foreign students. The Mexican-American variant differs from the main course only in having an additional reader that includes material of interest to Chicano students and relevant to the various themes. The individualized instruction variant meets as a regular class for the first several weeks, then is individ-

Figure 1: The Structure of Freshman English Courses at UT-Austin

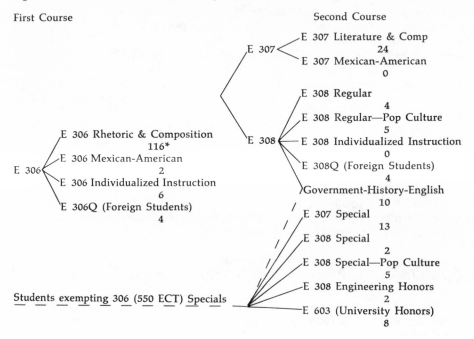

First Course

Second Course

E 306 Rhetoric & Composition
116*

E 306 Mexican-American
2

E 306 Individualized Instruction
6

E 306Q (Foreign Students)
4

E 307 Literature & Comp
24

E 307 Mexican-American
0

E 308 Regular
4

E 308 Regular—Pop Culture
5

E 308 Individualized Instruction
0

E 308Q (Foreign Students)
4

Government-History-English
10

E 307 Special
13

E 308 Special
2

E 308 Special—Pop Culture
5

E 308 Engineering Honors
2

E 603 (University Honors)
8

Students exempting 306 (550 ECT) Specials

* Indicates numbers of sections for that course for the fall semester, 1977.

ualized in laboratory meetings with undergraduate tutors and teachers; the course emphasizes initial grammar and sentence-combining work more than the regular course, although the students do whole themes at the end of the class. The E 306 II has not yet been used as a remedial course, but it may soon be given that orientation. The E 306Q courses do not emphasize writing and rhetorical skills as much as the regular course; speaking and grammar are also important elements of the course.

After E 306 the student takes one of the courses listed under *Second Course.* Only students exempting E 306 can take *special* courses listed in the lower half of the chart.

The four major courses offered under *Second Course* are E 307, E 308, GS 913, and E 603. All of these are basically composition courses with specified required writing assignments. (E 307 and E 308 require seven themes.) For mechanics, all of these courses use the handbook used in E 306. All but E 603 have a strong rhetorical syllabus, and all have anthologized readers or specified reading assignments. Indeed, it is the reading assignments that differentiate the courses. In all of the variants of E 307 the students read fictional materials (short stories and short novels) and write themes related to the readings. The kinds of themes required in the following units are, in order: an expressive autobiography or biography, a paper on fiction versus nonfiction unity (usually the rewrite of a myth to achieve a different aim), creating or analyzing a plot, creating or analyzing a character, an analytical paper emphasizing close reading of a text, a paper emphasizing library research, an evaluative paper. The E 308 courses generally emphasize nonbelletristic readings. The E 308 popular culture variant, for example, stresses current mass media scripts from contemporary speeches, radio and television broadcasts (documentaries, soap operas, etc.), Gonzo journalism, and so on. The themes focus on the following types of assignments: persuading (creative or analytical), advertising (creative or analytical), comparing or contrasting two reports of the same incident, describing or narrating in the style of the new journalism, presenting the same material in a traditional journalistic manner, defining a culture hero or describing a cultural pattern of behavior from an outsider's point of view, or persuading by means of an oral presentation to the class.

The readings in GS 913 are literary, historical, and theoretical. The English classes meet conjointly with required government and history classes, and the themes are closely correlated to the content demands of these two classes.

The readings in the engineering honors classes, E 308 EH, are both literary and scientific. Initially, the readings were preponderantly scientific, including classical and contemporary essays; but the students insisted on the inclusion of more literary materials.

The readings in E 603, the university honors course for both freshman composition and sophomore literature, are drawn from masterpieces in world literature. Often, though not necessarily, they follow a chronological sequence. The writing assignments differ more from instructor to instructor than in the other English classes.

Rhetorical Basis and Pedagogical Assumptions
Underlying Freshman Composition at UT Austin[1]

The freshman composition program at UT Austin has had a rhetorical foundation for a good number of years. At the present time, there is a systematic and articulated rhetorical basis for each of the three basic courses in the freshman program. Some of the more important principles underlying all three syllabuses are:

(1) There are specific rhetorical and mechanical skills which can be taught, at least at the level of ordinary workaday prose.

(2) The major teachable rhetorical skills relate to the different purposes for which we use language and the different general perspectives taken of subject matters. The major purposes for which we use language, the aims of discourse, are exposition (informing, proving and explaining, exploring), persuasion, literature, and self-expression. The major perspectives from which subject matters are viewed are classification and definition, narration, description, and evaluation.

These skills have to be differentiated in teaching, because they are fundamentally quite distinct. The criteria for effective propaganda (persuasion) are not at all the same criteria for effective literature or effective expository writing. Similarly, the criteria for a good narrative are quite dissimilar to those of classifying and defining.

It is quite true that these different aims often overlap in practice—as do different modes. But, just as tennis players spend hours practicing the serve and other hours practicing backhand and forehand volleys, so different skills are necessary to achieve overall competence in writing. And a person quite expert in one skill can be extremely deficient in another.

(3) These different skills cannot be taught all at once. Experience has demonstrated that we can learn them best by focusing on one major rhetorical skill analytically in a given theme and by relying on our already learned competencies instinctively with regard to other major skills. We have used all of these skills with some degree of confidence intuitively since childhood. Thus we have all told stories without an analytical awareness of the nature of narrative. In college, for the first time systematically, it is possible to improve these skills by a conscious analytic awareness of their processes.

(4) These skills are most successfully achieved when the writer says something he really believes in, for a specific purpose, to a well-defined audience. Therefore, individual choices of subject matter, especially in E 306 and E 308, and to some extent in E 307, are encouraged. This is an application of situational rhetoric to freshman composition.

In addition to a rhetorical basis, the program at UT Austin has also consciously followed some fairly well-established educational principles, a few of which are articulated below.

(1) A student learns to write by *writing*. Many students write as many as twelve themes a semester (counting revisions). Although anthologized readings, rhetorical principles, and handbook exercises may assist, they are not substitutes for the act of writing.

(2) A student learns to write by writing *whole* themes. There is a frankly holistic approach to writing. The whole themes may be quite short, even one-paragraph themes, but they should have something to say, a specific purpose, and a clearly defined audience.

(3) The teaching of mechanical skills (grammar, spelling, punctuation, kinds and registers of dialect, etc.) isolated from the actual writing of themes is not useful. The isolated teaching of rhetorical skills (such as library research, logic, and rhetoric) is almost equally useless.

Training Program for Teaching Assistants

In the fall of 1977, about seventy percent of the courses in the freshman program were taught by teaching assistants. About two thirds of these were graduate students in English; one third were graduate students in other areas such as linguistics, comparative literature, philosophy, English education, and so forth, but with B.A.'s or M.A.'s in English. Because of the preponderantly literary emphasis in their earlier degrees, most of these teaching assistants did not have the background necessary to teach some of these courses. Consequently, a training program was instituted to train new teaching assistants. The program contains an orientation program of one week prior to their first semester of teaching, an observing period of apprenticeship in which the inexperienced teaching assistant learns the syllabuses by working with a full-time faculty member but does not teach his own class, and two three-hour, semester-long courses, specifically related to the course that the beginning teacher is teaching his first two semesters. These graduate courses closely follow the syllabus of the course the beginning teacher is teaching, supplying the rhetorical basis for the lessons and suggesting practical techniques for handling the rhetoric, the readings, and the handbook exercises. The course tries to stay about a week ahead of the freshman courses to enable the beginning teacher to prepare ahead of time. This requires a close synchronization of all teaching assistants in the syllabus sequence when they take the teacher-training course. Afterward they may depart from the syllabus.

Teaching assistants' reaction to the training program has progressed from resentful compliance to enthusiastic reception. Some older teaching assistants who were not required to follow the training program now follow all or part of the teacher-training courses. And some full-time faculty participate in the orientation program and parts of the courses in teacher training. To date, eight different faculty members have taught the training course.

Besides the faculty contribution to the training program, older experienced teaching assistants act as counselors to the incoming teaching assistants. Six or seven new teaching assistants are assigned to each counselor. He or she meets with these new teachers in a group once or twice a week, observes them once or twice during the semester, and helps them in grading, lesson preparation, and personal problems. The counselor component of the training program is possibly the single most valuable component of the training sequence.

Weaknesses in the Program

Although the program at UT Austin has experienced continual growth and improvement over the past fifteen years, there are still some obvious deficiencies. For this reason, the Freshman English Policy Committee, a group of four faculty members and four teaching assistants, is continually experimenting with innovative suggestions that question either the procedural matters of the syllabuses or the very basis of the courses. Experimental suggestions are requested every semester and tested with whatever research facilities are available to the program. Experiments usually involve pre- and post-tests and a minimum regard for research design. This semester six different programs are being tested by these criteria.

We are now attempting to eliminate grade inflation (partly arising from required student evaluations), to provide an intelligent rationale for the sequence from first-semester to second-semester freshman courses to sophomore literature courses, and to make provisions for minority students whose performance is weak.

Notes

[1] The rhetorical principles outlined in this section can be found articulated in detail, with evidence and documentation, in James L. Kinneavy, *A Theory of Discourse: The Aims of Discourse* (Englewood Cliffs, N.J.: Prentice-Hall, 1971). A less scholarly presentation of the aims of discourse, intended for upper-division undergraduate students, can be seen in James L. Kinneavy, John W. Cope, and J. W. Campbell, *Aims and Audiences in Writing* (Dubuque, Iowa: Kendall/Hunt, 1976).

The Freshman Composition Program at Arizona State University

Frank J. D'Angelo, Director of Freshman Composition

Department responsible for the composition program   English
Full-time faculty in the department   49
Enrollment policies
    Maximum Enrollment   25
    Minimum Enrollment   N/A
    Average Enrollment   25
Staffing
    Percentage of freshman composition courses taught by graduate students   90
    Percentage taught by part-time faculty (excluding graduate students)   2
    Percentage taught by assistant, associate, and/or full professors   8
Program size
    Number of students enrolled in the freshman composition program in the fall term of 1976   3,450
    Number of sections of freshman composition offered in the fall term of 1976   138
    Number of sections at all levels—literature, composition, film, graduate, undergraduate, etc.—offered by the department in the fall term of 1976   321

When I arrived at Arizona State University in 1970, the freshman English program had a clearly defined shape and direction, despite the rapid changes brought about by the political and social dissatisfaction of the mid- and late sixties. This is not to say that there was no room for improvement. It is to say, however, that the department did not succumb to the sway of "relevance" or to the pressure of doing away with freshman English requirements entirely.

The freshman English requirements today at Arizona State University are the same as they were in the sixties, although the composition program has changed somewhat. All students who expect to graduate with a baccalaureate degree under any curriculum of Arizona State University must take a minimum of three hours of freshman composition (En 104—"Advanced First Year English") or a maximum of six hours of freshman English (En 101–En 102—"Freshman English"). Eligibility to take En 104 instead of En 101 and 102 is determined by the student's ACT verbal score or by his or her performance on a departmental exemption examination. All students whose ACT verbal scores are of the ninety-second percentile or above automatically go into En 104. Students whose ACT scores are between the eighty-second and the ninety-first percentiles are eligible to take a two-hour essay examination. Those who pass this exam go into En 104. All other students must take En 101 and En 102.

In addition to these two ways of bypassing En 101 and 102, the English department provides incoming students with a third alternative. Those students who do well in EN 101 may, upon recommendation of the instructor, take an essay exam at the end of the semester; if they pass the exam, they are exempt from taking En 102 and are considered to have fulfilled the freshman English requirements.

Besides the university's general education requirements, the College of Liberal Arts requires that all of its students receive a C or better in En 101 and En 102, or En 104. Students who make less than a C in these courses are presumed not to have demonstrated the necessary degree of writing proficiency required of a graduate of the College of Liberal Arts. Therefore, such students must successfully complete a written English proficiency exam, which must be taken during the semester immediately following the completion of any of the courses in which they failed to receive an acceptable grade. Students who do not complete the examination successfully on the first try must enroll in an English course prescribed by the Director of Freshman English. Students who receive a grade of C or better in such a course will be considered to have satisfied the proficiency requirement. Otherwise, they must repeat the above procedure until they have demonstrated the necessary degree of writing proficiency.

For poorly prepared students, the English department has a number of options. First, there are special sections of freshman English for minority students, taught by instructors (Indian, Mexican-American, black, etc.) who are sensitive to the linguistic and social needs of such students. Second, there are special classes for foreign students, taught by faculty and graduate students who have some expertise in teaching English as a second language. Finally, there is a writing clinic to which any student can be referred for tutorial help.

The freshman English courses are taught almost exclusively by graduate students. Perhaps ten percent of the classes are taught by professors on the permanent staff or by part-time instructors. To prepare teaching assistants for their teaching responsibilities, the department requires all new teaching assistants to attend three-day orientation sessions the week before classes begin in the fall and to enroll in a seminar in the teaching of composition taught by the Director of Freshman English.

In the orientation sessions, members of the professorial staff, who are frequently members of the Freshman English Committee, give a series of presentations on such topics as effective theme assignments, evaluating student themes, and proper use of the texts. In the teaching assistants' seminar, the TAs are introduced to such basic concepts as the relationship between rhetoric and composition, invention, arrangement, style, modes of discourse, audience, and critical reading.

The objectives of the freshman English course are stated in the *Freshman English Handbook* as follows: "First Year English is designed to improve the reading and writing skills of the freshman student. Its aim is to give the student the skills he or she will need to function as a reader and writer of English at the University level." To this stated aim, the Freshman English Committee has recently added another: "To get students to bring to their writing a self-conscious awareness of the part that thinking plays in the composing process."

The structure of the course has changed since the early sixties. At that time, and up until 1973, En 101 was based upon the traditional modes of discourse: description, narration, exposition, and argumentation. In En 102, the emphasis was on writing about literature and style. In 1973, however, the Freshman English Committee decided to make a major change in the program.

The theoretical foundation for the modes of discourse approach was the ideas of Alexander Bain and William B. Cairns.[1] But some committee members argued that the traditional approach to the modes of discourse was based on an outworn faculty psychology and therefore needed to be discarded. (According to Alexander Bain, the forms of discourse are the kinds of composition that relate to the faculties of the mind. Thus, description, narration, and exposition relate to the faculty of understanding, and persuasion relates to the will.)

There was no explicit theoretical foundation for En 102, although implicit in the idea of having students write themes about literature was the formalist conception of close reading and critical analysis. But more often than not, many graduate students assumed they were teaching an introductory course in literature rather than a course in composition, and the teaching of writing suffered.

The theoretical foundation for restructuring both En 101 and En 102 came from certain ideas that later appeared in an article entitled "The Search for Intelligible Structure in the Teaching of Composition."[2] The thesis of the article is that, although composition (like classical rhetoric) does not have a specific content, it does have an underlying structure, which gives unity and coherence to the field; and that such a structure can be conceived of in terms of principles and forms. The principles are linguistic (coordination, subordination, predication, complementation, modification) and rhetorical (invention, arrangement, style). The forms are the modes or kinds of discourse.

En 101 is based on the principles of composition. En 102 is based on the kinds of discourse.

In addition to the overall theoretical structure provided by the "Search for Intelligible Structure," En 101 also uses as a theoretical framework a number of ideas set forth in two fairly recent books.[3] The thesis in both of these books is that invention, arrangement, and style are parts of an organic whole that are related to underlying thought processes.

Although the Freshman English Committee is fairly well satisfied with the theoretical basis for En 101, there is no attempt to impose a single format on the entire program. Instead it was decided to allow for as much flexibility as possible by incorporating the basic principles into abstract outlines that represent three organized methods for covering the material: "From the Whole to the Parts," "From the Parts to the Whole," and "Patterns of Development."

The approach entitled "From the Whole to the Parts" has three main divisions: prewriting, organization, and style. The prewriting section is further subdivided into sections dealing with the writer, the writer's purpose, his or her audience, the subject, and probing for ideas. The section on organization treats such concerns as formulating a thesis; indicating a plan of development; considering kinds of introductions and conclusions; logical, chronological, and spatial orders; and continuity and transitions. Paragraphs and paragraphing are handled as a part of larger organizational concerns. The section on style deals with grammatical and rhetorical sentence types and with diction and usage.

The approach entitled "From the Parts to the Whole" is not merely the inverse of "From the Whole to the Parts." This approach is based on an extension of the work of Francis Christensen with the rhetoric of the sentence and the paragraph.[4] Teachers using this approach begin with the grammar and rhetoric of the sentence, and with the cumulative sentence as a special sentence type. Then an analogy is made between the sentence and the paragraph, with the cumulative sentence handled as an embryonic paragraph. The paragraph in turn is treated as a macrocosmic cumulative sentence. Next an analogy is made between the paragraph and the essay. In this analogy, the paragraph is an essay in microcosm and, conversely, the essay is a macrocosmic paragraph. This approach to the teaching of composition relies heavily on grammatical principles, while incorporating aspects of the patterns of development.

The final approach, "Patterns of Development," considers the so-called "methods of development" (analysis, classification, definition, comparison, cause and effect, and so forth) as both heuristic and organizational. That is, categories such as analysis, comparison, and cause and effect are conceived of as topics of invention and as patterns of arrangement. In their paradigmatic form, these patterns of arrangement are structural counterparts of *topoi*.[5]

There is, of course, much more that could be said about these approaches. What I have presented is an outline, highlighting the central features of each approach. The intent of isolating the grammatical and rhetorical principles of discourse from the modes of discourse (the modes are not neglected in En 101, but assumed) is to place the emphasis more fully on composition as process, rather than on composition as product. In En 102, students are expected to apply these grammatical and rhetorical principles in their own writing and in their critical reading and analyses of the modes of discourse.

The emphasis in En 102, then, is on the kinds or modes of discourse. The theoretical foundation of this approach is based very loosely on recent scholarship dealing with the modes of discourse.[6]

The basic work of En 102 is a series of themes that expose the student to fundamental problems of reading and writing about printed material. When students reach En 102, the instructor should not have to go back and teach the fundamental principles and skills that students should have gotten in En 101. In En 102, the teacher should *expect* students to begin applying grammatical and rhetorical principles to their critical reading and writing about kinds of discourse.

I have stated that the kinds of writing students attend to in En 102 are the modes of discourse, very loosely conceived. The two main kinds of writing focused upon are literary discourse and popular writing (advertising, newspaper articles, magazine articles, and popular novels). In dealing with one or the other of these kinds of writing, the instructor may organize the course by devoting successive segments of it to two basic kinds of assignments: looking at one work (some means of expressing ideas and attitudes) and looking at several works.

In looking at a single work, students are asked to explore the features that various kinds of discourse have in common. For example, in analyzing form and structure, they are asked to consider the organizational patterns in nonfiction prose, the plot in fiction, or the "logic" of poetry. Similarly, in studying point of view, students are reminded that all kinds of writing have a point of view: the writer's in nonfiction, the narrator's in fiction, and the speaker's in poetry. Or, for instance, the setting in fiction may be related to the rhetorical context in nonfiction prose. In addition to analyzing structure, point of view, setting, or rhetorical context, students are asked to focus on the theme of a literary work or the thesis of an essay. Finally, they may be asked to analyze style. In analyzing style, they are asked to look at a stylistic device as being both unique to a particular kind of discourse and applicable to all kinds of discourse. (For instance, figures of speech may be viewed as literary devices or as signs of basic assumptions in exposition or argument.)

In looking at several works, students are asked to compare the form or structure of two works, two contrasting points of view, two ideas, two characters, and so forth, so that there is an explicit tie-in with the kinds of features they have been asked to analyze when looking at a single work. Looking at several works leads students naturally to the research paper, a project in which they are asked to gather views and information, review opinions, and synthesize the results into a coherent whole.

The En 104 course combines features of En 101 and En 102, with a heavier emphasis on the readings than on the basic compositional skills. Obviously, the selection of texts for EN 104 differs from the selection of texts for En 101 and En 102.

As with all programs, the freshman composition program at Arizona State University has its weaknesses. Its strength, however, is that there is at least some attempt to present students with a logical sequence of principles and forms, ensuring a close fit between what they get in En 101 and what they get in En 102. If the program seems a bit rigid, it is because the department feels that many students coming to the university have simply not had the kinds of writing experiences and mastered the skills in high school that they should have. Naturally, the Freshman English Committee and the department as a whole are constantly reviewing the curriculum, with an eye toward instituting changes whenever these seem desirable.

Notes

[1] See Frank J. D'Angelo, "Modes of Discourse," in *Teaching Composition: 10 Bibliographical Essays*, ed. Gary Tate (Fort Worth: Texas Christian University Press, 1977), pp. 111–35.

[2] *College Composition and Communication*, 27 (May 1976), 142–47.

[3] Frank D'Angelo, *A Conceptual Theory of Rhetoric* (Cambridge, Mass.: Winthrop, 1975), and, *Process and Thought in Composition* (Cambridge, Mass.: Winthrop, 1977).

[4] Francis Christensen, *Notes toward a New Rhetoric* (New York: Harper & Row, 1967).

[5] See "Paradigms as Structural Counterparts of *Topoi*," forthcoming in *Language and Style*, in a special issue on composition.

[6] For a topographical survey, see D'Angelo, "Modes of Discourse."

Freshman English at Ohio State University

Susan Miller, Director of Freshman English

Department responsible for the composition program   English
Full-time faculty in the department   68
Enrollment policies
    Maximum Enrollment   24
    Minimum Enrollment   12
    Average Enrollment   23
Staffing
    Percentage of freshman composition courses taught by graduate students   92
    Percentage taught by part-time faculty (excluding graduate students)   3
    Percentage taught by full-time instructors or lecturers   2
    Percentage taught by assistant, associate, and/or full professors   3
Program size
    Number of students enrolled in the freshman composition program in the fall term of 1976   3,095
    Number of sections of freshman composition offered in the fall term of 1976   130
    Number of sections at all levels—literature, composition, film, graduate, undergraduate, etc.—offered by the department in the fall term of 1976   253

Ohio State University's freshman program is distinguished by being at once the largest and smallest of its kind. That is, over 7,500 students are instructed each year in the one one-quarter course required by each of the colleges of the university, English 110. Some of this number (approximately 1,500 students) are placed in either one or two quarters of a prerequisite remedial workshop that opened in the fall of 1977. Considerations of quantity are, then, the keys to understanding the qualities of the program: both the enormous numbers of students served and the miniscule time allowed to instruct them greatly influence what is done.

Changes that characterize the fortunes of freshman English across the country have molded the recent history of the program at Ohio State. From 1951 to 1971, three quarters of composition were required by each of the colleges of the university. After national test scores started rising and some of the colleges decided to stop requiring the third quarter of the sequence, the department of English—always overburdened by the administration of this series—voted in 1970 to replace the three courses with one five-hour course. This one-quarter course, plus a two-course, six-hour sequence sponsored by Developmental Education for Freshman Foundation Program students as a substitute option, was the only writing course taught at the freshman level from 1971 until 1977. Then, in response to the declining scores and student performance widely noted by teachers throughout the university, a remedial program of either two quarters (for students whose ACT scores are 1–10 in English) or one quarter (for those whose scores are 11–15) was begun in the fall of 1977. The workshop has been funded for four years; the university hopes that high-school instruction will improve and finally eliminate the need for this pre-university preparation.

Placement is controlled not only by scores at the lower end of the scale but also by achievement, which allows the student to receive EM (Examination) credit for English 110. Students scoring 26 and above on the ACT examination receive such credit; those scoring 24 and 25 may take a proficiency examination for the same credit. (Approximately 12% of those who take the test receive credit for the course.) Transfer students who enter with only three credits of composition must pass the same examination to avoid the course. Consequently, the majority of students instructed each year represent the middle range on the ACT test, with scores from 16 to 23.

The theoretical bases of this course have only lately been stated. Teachers of writing at Ohio State believe that writing can be taught, that a writing course is a process rather than only content or material to be learned, and that their greatest strength, considering the diversity of their and their students' interests, is sharing their own writing processes in the context of a carefully sequenced developmental class. The program emphasizes the importance of building rather than "making" assignments, and each teacher is encouraged to instruct students in prewriting techniques that are appropriate to each organizational pattern practiced in the course. Revision, editing, and proofreading are taught separately; many teachers do not grade (as opposed to comment upon) revised student papers until the final weeks of a quarter. The movement from the process of composing to the product finally "published" is the basis for the course and all of its assignments.

In 1976 the Freshman English Policy Committee, an elected representative group of staff members and students who advise the director, defined the goals of English 110 in the following terms. The course is "an enabling course which not only teaches conventions of using and editing but also teaches the whole process of writing." The course emphasizes the expository forms demanded in college writing and the processes that lead to them. Its teachers, who are rarely criticized by the university community for failing to do what a one-quarter course cannot do, also stated their hope that beginning instruction would be continued by teachers in the students' other courses. Research about reasonable expectations of change in student writing controls the realization on the part of most of the staff that they can only begin a long process and should not expect dramatic long-term improvement to result from one ten-week course.

At the same time that they stated the goals of 110, the Policy Committee also agreed upon a statement of minimal standards for a grade of C that focuses on the quality of edited, revised themes and of reading skills. Many teachers have found these standards a supportive tool for combating grade inflation. Although approximately fifty percent of the students enrolled in English 110 received A or B grades in 1976–77, grades are less inflated than they were a few years ago.

English 110 can probably best be characterized as a "C Major" survey of college composition. Students are required to write two paragraphs and six themes, at least three of which may be revised before final grading. No long research paper is required, but many teachers ask for a documented essay and spend time acquainting the students with library resources. Beginning teachers use a prescribed syllabus and a rhetoric and reader selected by the director in consultation with the Freshman English Policy Committee; after the first quarter, teachers may choose from a list of approved rhetorics, readers, and handbooks. None of these books offers many surprises. Teachers are firmly discouraged from including literature as either reading material or the subject of writing assignments since expository reading and writing are to be fostered. Students who wish to may elect a freshman-level "Introduction to Literature," a three-hour course taught primarily at present by instructors and by graduate teaching associates who have passed their Ph.D. qualifying exams.

All of this is not to say that no experimentation or innovation occurs within the program. Each quarter, two or three sections of English 110 use films in conjunction with a rhetoric text to explain analogies between written and visual media. In 1976 a section of English 110 was offered for music majors; its materials included music criticism, and its assignments were especially adapted to the writing these students regularly do. Three teachers of English 110 worked one quarter with faculty in classics, philosophy, and comparative literature as instructors of separate, parallel writing courses. In addition, a number of teachers regularly elect to rate holistically a final examination provided for them so that a small percentage of their students' grades come from another reliable source. Many teachers who wish to try a new text or innovative approach to teaching do so after consulting with the director.

The staff also has available a number of resources that support teaching in addition to close supervision during an initial training quarter. Since classes are taught in two widely separated campuses, secretarial help and a resources room (containing catalogued texts, articles, journals, and proven exercises) are provided at each location. The Undergraduate English Forum in 1975 began a tutorial service for English 110 students, which has been carefully supervised so that tutors are well trained to aid instruction. The department maintains a videotaping service for teachers who wish to have classes recorded. Each year a staff member is selected by the Freshman English Policy Committee to receive a nonteaching appointment as Freshman English Ombudsman. This person hears complaints from students confidentially and works to keep communication between teachers and students open so that only persistent or extraordinary problems must be arbitrated by the director. At least twice a year, the editorial board of *Moreover* (the first word of a famous plagiarized theme) publishes an in-house journal that includes exchanges about debatable pedagogical issues, book reviews, and discussions of new ideas and information. The Dean of the College of Humanities sets aside one thousand dollars each year to be divided among those teachers the FEPC selects for the Freshman English Distinguished Teaching Award.

The vast majority of teachers of freshman writing are teaching associates, who made up ninety-two percent of the staff in 1977. As literature enrollments continue to decline, however, this percentage will fall; just this year, in fact, regular faculty have been asked to indicate which of the lower- or upper-level writing courses (in expository writing, critical writing, or technical writing) they would prefer to teach, and a projected new Arts and Sciences required junior-level writing course will undoubtedly increase the number of faculty who teach a writing course. Even so, most teachers of freshman English are teaching associates who began teaching concurrently with beginning graduate study. From 1965 till 1976, new teachers were required to take a graduate course (for credit) designed to guide them through their first quarter of teaching as well as to acquaint them with useful resources in composition. Because of long-term dissatisfaction with the course on the part of many graduate students, the faculty voted in the spring of 1977 to require a one-quarter weekly workshop for new teachers and another elected course in rhetoric, composition theory, or language study to be taken during the first year of teaching. New teachers must, then, attend a week of orientation workshops before classes begin, attend weekly workshops during their first quarter of teaching, and take some related course during their first year on the staff. Teachers in the remedial workshop must be experienced English 110 teachers who volunteer and who first take a graduate-level course designed especially for them.

Since the assignment of a course involves complete and independent responsibility for the conduct of the class and the grading of students, teachers of freshman English are regularly evaluated by criteria similar to those applied to any faculty member. They must submit their individual syllabus to the director by the second week of each quarter, must be visited in class at least once during their first two years of teaching, and must each year submit a summary of student evaluations of one of their classes. While the Director of Freshman English is responsible for these evaluative procedures, staff members are neither selected nor terminated (when that is rarely necessary) by the director. Teaching associates are appointed by the department chairman, acting on the recommendation of the Graduate Committee, and they are subject to contractual obligations and procedures that apply to all university personnel. Their salaries and schedules are administered by the department chairman.

With so large a staff at various stages of graduate work and professional life, the department's "approach" to composition offers a microcosm of the entire profession's predispositions. An active group of graduate students has recently become interested in teaching a research-based writing course guided by the best new information available about the writing process, evaluation, and reasonable expectations of a beginning writer. The remedial program was not implemented, for instance, until a year of research and testing in a pilot project could support the claim that such a program would in fact improve student writing. Another group, influenced by the politics of the sixties and early seventies, sees composition classes as human growth settings and continues to emphasize social, political, and moral issues as writing topics. Yet another small group clings to the belief that learning to read literature can turn inexperienced freshmen into competent writers.

All in all, this diversity has kept vital and changing what might well have become inert and monstrous. No faction or clique dominates decision-making within the Policy Committee or the faculty, yet the departmental statements about the objectives and standards in freshman English courses prevent most student charges against unreasonable variation in the content, conduct, or grading of the course. The university supports the program by acknowledging the dedication with which its teachers approach a difficult job; many non-English faculty have participated in workshops designed to help them assign and evaluate successfully the writing in their own courses. Everyone agrees that more courses in writing are now needed, but no one questions the constraints that sheer numbers place on implementing and supporting any expansion of the program.

The Graduate Student Teacher-Training Program at the University of Missouri, Columbia

Winifred B. Horner, Chairman of Lower Division Studies

Department responsible for the composition program   English
Full-time faculty in the department   41
Enrollment policies
      Maximum Enrollment   22
      Minimum Enrollment   15
      Average Enrollment   20
Staffing
      With the exception of the two tenured faculty members who direct the program, the entire composition staff is made up of graduate students.
Program size
      Number of students enrolled in the freshman composition program in the fall term of 1976   1,131
      Number of sections of freshman composition offered in the fall term of 1976   52
      Number of sections at all levels—literature, composition, film, graduate, undergraduate, etc.—offered by the department in the fall term of 1976   305

The University of Missouri maintains a composition program coordinated by two regular faculty members hired specifically for that purpose, one whose specialty is rhetoric and linguistics and the other whose specialty is Renaissance rhetoric. The writing courses are taught by a staff of approximately one hundred graduate students, who are required to take a course in language theory in their first semester and, in that and subsequent semesters, are supported by a writing resource library and by two supervisors who visit their classes and consult with them on course plans, paper-marking, and any problems that may come up in their teaching. The composition program supports and enriches a healthy graduate program, which produces Ph.D.'s and M.A.'s with experience and skill in teaching, and with some knowledge of rhetorical history, linguistic research, contemporary language theories, and dialectology, in addition to literature.

The English department serves thirteen colleges and divisions: Agriculture, Arts and Science, Business and Public Administration, Education, Engineering, Home Economics, Journalism, Law, Library and Information Science, Medicine, Nursing, Public and Community Services, and Veterinary Medicine. Though each college or division determines its own writing requirements, for the most part the requirement is one of the following three courses (or groups of courses), as determined by the students' rank in their high-school class in conjunction with their scores on the Missouri College English Test and the School and College Aptitude Test. Those in the lower fifty percent of the freshman class must take English 1 and English 60; those in the middle thirty-five percent take only English 60; and those in the upper fifteen percent take English 65 GH. English 1, not a remedial course, is the basic college composition course required of all students not testing into another course. (English 1-IS is the ESL equivalent of English 1.) English 60 is a *sophomore* level course designed to improve the writing skills of those who have passed, or tested out of, English 1. English 65 GH is designed for exceptionally well prepared freshmen who have demonstrated their qualifications through entrance examination scores and through high-school rank; though it is a one-semester course, it carries six hours' credit toward graduation.

Through the 1950s and 1960s the University of Missouri staffed most of its freshman and sophomore writing and literature courses with graduate students. Of the nearly twenty courses in lower-division studies, almost all used some graduate students as teachers; the composition courses used only graduate students. But what was considered a weakness of the program in the sixties has turned out, through farsighted department leadership, to be the strength of the program in the seventies. The composition program, by affording financial support to graduate students, is the bulwark that, quite literally, supports the graduate program. It further supports the graduate program by providing strong candidates in the present tight job market. They are strong because they have, in addition to their literary expertise, wide teaching experience and a skill and interest in teaching writing. In the past five years the graduate program has shifted from a large Ph.D. program to one made up of a few highly qualified Ph.D. students and a large group of well-qualified M.A. students, who are selected from a sizable group of applicants. The shift has been gradual, steady, and healthy.

In addition, and more important, the quality of the teaching in the composition courses has improved in the seventies. Indeed, *because* there are so many new M.A.'s acting as TAs, the department and the university feel bound to maintain a strong support program in the first year of teaching. In the department, that means faculty support for a required graduate course in rhetoric and linguistics; in the university administration that means financial support for two full-time faculty members in rhetoric and small classes that range from sixteen to twenty-two students. As a result, new teaching assistants, whether M.A. or Ph.D. candidates, no longer walk into the composition class not knowing what to teach and longing only to get through with composition and into the real business of teaching literature. As enrollments in literature courses continue to decline, graduate students recognize the teaching of writing as part of a lifelong commitment, not just through necessity but increasingly through clear first choice. More important, as they trace the broad outlines of the history of rhetoric in their course work, they see themselves as part of a long tradition that goes back to ancient Greece. Finally, they recognize that their expertise in the teaching of composition may well be the decisive factor in securing a position when they graduate.

Composition programs stand at the heart of the English discipline and have changed and been changed by concurrent alterations in graduate programs. The health of one, in large measure, has determined the health of the other, and at the University of Missouri the health of both is good. But such has not always been the case.

In 1971 the English graduate studies chairman noticed the small enrollments in the M.A. program and initiated a drive to attract more and better M.A. students. He sent letters to schools around the country, but response was meager since there was no financial support to offer these students. As a result, he suggested that a few of the best qualified M.A. students be allowed to teach one section of freshman composition, a proposition that old hands regarded as destructive to the teaching program.

Having always been proud that only Ph.D. students were allowed to teach freshman composition, the English department faculty often ignored the darker side of the system: some TAs had been allowed to teach two, three, and even four sections of freshman English; with a load of one hundred students per semester, they read, commented on, and graded one hundred themes each week. Along with this load, they were expected to work toward a Ph.D. degree.

The results were predictable: those teaching assistants who survived the first year divided themselves into two widely separated groups. Some spent their time on freshman composition, piling up delayed grades in their course work and hanging on for years, often outlasting their own professors; others spent their time on course work, neglecting their teaching and becoming adept at all the necessary shortcuts that, in the long run, shortcut their students. The graduate students who survived the initial years and did well in their course work were rewarded by being assigned literature courses, which they were, after all, qualified to teach and which, at that time, they fully expected to teach for the rest of their lives. Composition was forever behind them. Freshman English, then, each year, was turned over to a new group of incoming Ph.D. students and to those graduate students who had dropped out of the program or who were not progressing in their course work. In many cases, teaching assistants quietly abandoned their graduate work or maintained the appearance of graduate work by taking one or two courses a year, committing their real efforts to full-time teaching. The addition of M.A. students to the instructional staff of the composition course seemed to offer little hope for improvement in an already unhealthy situation. In the fifties and sixties such a situation was not atypical and has been documented by Albert Kitzhaber, among others, as common at many large universities. It is still not unusual today.

At the University of Missouri the influx of M.A. students in the seventies gradually affected the makeup of the teaching staff, ultimately improving the quality of the teaching in the composition course. As the number of graduate students who were teaching increased, the teaching load of each teaching assistant necessarily had to decrease to accommodate that number. New master's students were allowed to teach only one section of composition in their first year and two sections in the second—if their teaching record was good and their progress in the graduate program was satisfactory. Thus, at the present time, all new teaching assistants assume a reasonable teaching load in their first semester of graduate work—only one section for M.A.'s with no prior teaching experience, and no more than two sections for anyone.

A second change brought about by the new plan was the quality of the graduate student TAs. Even minimal financial support increased the number of M.A. applicants, and selection of teaching assistants became highly competitive. Of the students admitted to the program only the best were asked to teach.

A third benefit came from the university academic support program designed to help the new teaching assistants. Money was granted to establish a resource file of teaching materials, and a small private donation was used to set up an instructional library for the freshman English staff. The library includes a file of materials with over thirty categories of sample course plans, exams, theme assignments, and appropriate exercises.

A fourth benefit was the establishment of a course in rhetorical theory as a requirement for every new teacher. Historically, the department had maintained a good supervision program, a model in its time. Two or three half-time supervisors had visited teachers' classes, checked course plans, consulted on paper-marking and grading, and conducted a three-day preschool workshop. Also, new teachers had taken a course in the problems of teaching composition. The course was good in theory but had major flaws in practice. Since it could be audited and was not required, all teaching assistants audited. Therefore, reading could not be assigned, attendance could not be enforced, and, consequently, the course lacked serious content. Most class sessions revolved around an exchange of ideas, most of them not new or original, and long discussions of individual teaching problems, often silly or trivial ("I have a student named Miss Sex, and everytime I call the roll, the class laughs. What should I do?"). Furthermore, as graduate work increased during the first semester, attendance became more and more sporadic and the class was usually abandoned by Thanksgiving at the latest.

Thus, with the increasing number of M.A. students teaching, in 1974, the department instituted a graduate course entitled "Rhetorical and Linguistic

Theory Applied to the Teaching of English Language" as a requirement for all new teaching assistants. The course carried three hours of graduate credit. As more and more job descriptions asked for rhetoric and linguistics, the popularity of the course increased because graduate students wanted to have the course on their transcripts. And it is this course that has seriously changed the nature of the composition program at the University of Missouri. As students in the course examine contemporary theories of invention or Rogerian argument, they see composition as vastly more than the study of spelling, punctuation, and paragraph writing; as they trace the rhetorical tradition, they see rhetoric as the study of how one uses and is used by one's language, and they learn that rhetoric belongs at the center of the English discipline.

In the year of its inception, both beginning M.A. and Ph.D. students enrolled in the course, but subsequently the course has been taught in two sections—one for M.A.'s and one for Ph.D.'s. Both courses have similar basic requirements and use Corbett's *Classical Rhetoric* and William Labov's *Study of Nonstandard English*. Both groups of students read Aristotle's *Rhetoric*, a treatise that is far less familiar to English students than the *Poetics*. Ph.D. students spend more time on historical rhetoric, concentrating on their own period of specialization. M.A. students, who are usually novice teachers, spend more time fulfilling assignments connected with their teaching responsibilities, such as two-week course plans and theme guides. Both M.A. and Ph.D. students study contemporary theories of rhetoric, and both classes spend two weeks on language variation and methods of dealing with minority dialects in the writing course.

The general course requirements for new master's students include a fifteen-to-twenty-page paper on some rhetorical or linguistic theory applied to the teaching of composition or an annotated bibliography on some aspect of the teaching of writing, a one- or two-page evaluation of a contemporary textbook, and a syllabus for the course they are assigned to teach the following semester. There is an examination on the readings, which include, among others, excerpts from the works of Richard Young, Alton Becker, Kenneth Pike, James Kinneavy, Frank D'Angelo, S. I. Hayakawa, Francis Christensen, Stephen Toulmin, and William Labov.

Doctoral students, on the other hand, have the choice of doing a paper on some aspect of rhetoric in their period or on some language theory that interests them. They also prepare an annotated bibliography of their subject. In daily assignments they read more of the primary sources than do the M.A. students. Their reading includes Plato's *Phaedrus* and *Gorgias*, Aristotle's *Rhetoric*, and Book IV of *On Christian Doctrine*, and may include reports on such diversified modern writers as Richard Weaver, Carl Rogers, or John Searle. More than for the M.A. students, the emphasis is on the philosophical problems and the varied uses of language. Classroom application comes into the discussion, but the emphasis is on language theory.

The course also allows TAs to avoid the usual procedure of slogging painfully through the textbook one day ahead of the students. When the teacher approaches classification, he can present the tagmemic approach of contrast, distribution, and variation or Kenneth Pike's theory of particle, wave, and field. In teaching sentences he can use Strong or Christensen or a combination of the two. He may present argument from the viewpoint of Aristotle's enthymeme or the more modern Toulmin approach. He cannot bring all of his knowledge into the freshman composition course, but at least he has options.

The second result of the required course for new teachers is that composition gains a new legitimacy in the eyes of the graduate students. Composition is still recognized as the hardest course to teach, but it is no longer always thought of as a course taught only by second-class citizens. At least, those who know the tradition find it hard to place Aristotle in that category. Seeing composition as part of a tradition that goes back to ancient Greece and the study of English literature as a nineteenth-century innovation makes new teaching assistants stand taller in the composition classroom. Their knowledge of the rhetorical tradition allows them to see the teaching of composition and the study of literature as two sides of the rhetorical coin rather than as two separate disciplines.

Too often economic pressures and the demands of the job market limit our options and take us in directions we do not always choose. For the composition program at the University of Missouri, such has not been the case. The demand for teachers of writing and the social and economic necessity for improving writing skills in the general population have resulted in a new interest in the composition program and a new interest in linguistic and rhetorical research—an interest shared by most graduate students, many members of the English department faculty, and virtually all of the university community. Such interest has fortunately translated into academic and financial support for a strong and vital writing program.

The Freshman Composition Program at the University of Washington

William F. Irmscher, Director of Freshman English

Department responsible for the composition program   English
Full-time faculty in the department   63
Enrollment policies
  Maximum Enrollment   26
  Minimum Enrollment   10
  Average Enrollment   25
Staffing
  Percentage of freshman composition courses taught by graduate students   85
  Percentage taught by part-time faculty (excluding graduate students)   15
Program size
  Number of students enrolled in the freshman composition program in the fall term of 1976   1,944
  Number of sections of freshman composition offered in the fall term of 1976   79
  Number of sections at all levels—literature, composition, film, graduate, undergraduate, etc.—offered by the department in the fall term of 1976   190

Until 1968, the University of Washington had a university-wide require-ment of three quarters of freshman English. The department of English offered 101, 102, and 103, a typical sequence for all students who could qualify by passing the placement examination, and a remedial course, English N–50, for those who could not. In the peak year of 1965, we offered 197 sections of all courses.

In 1968, when the writing requirement was dropped by the College of Arts and Sciences, other colleges followed suit, although Forestry, Fisheries, Pharmacy, Nursing, and some individual departments of Arts and Sciences retained the requirement. For all practical purposes, however, freshman En-glish became an elective course. In the fall of 1969, the total number of sections had fallen to 120, but it was apparent that freshman English did not die for lack of a requirement.

The elimination of the requirement and the desire to attract students to beginning courses in writing prompted the department to rethink its freshman offerings. English 101, 102, and 103 had followed a pattern familiar in many colleges. English 101 offered practice in writing short analytical themes based upon essays by established writers; English 102 was a research-paper course; English 103 offered further practice, but writing was based on readings of imaginative literature. Quite obviously, all full-time faculty members, who at that time were required to teach at least one section of freshman English each year, consistently chose 103 as their teaching assignment.

In planning the restructured program, we began with a new premise. The old sequence had offered students only one approach to writing. All students moved lockstep through three courses; the courses were uniform. The funda-mental premise of the new program was that we would offer varying ap-proaches to writing, and students would choose the one they considered compatible with their interests. Our standard sequence had strongly empha-sized imaginative literature. Even 101 and 102, as well as the 103 course, included fiction and drama, thematically arranged, so that students could compare factual statement and literary statement on the same issues. Yet many students did not share the faculty's enthusiasm for the analysis of liter-ary works in a writing course that they viewed in far more utilitarian terms. Thus, in planning a new program, we thought of *ways* of teaching composi-tion, not *one* way. We decided upon one block of courses that would be reading/writing courses, a second block that would be what we have come to call "straight" writing courses—essentially courses that use student writing for analysis and only brief prose selections by established writers for purposes of illustration—and a third block designed especially for students admitted to the University under the Educational Opportunity Program.

The reading/writing courses place particular emphasis upon the generative stage of writing, on the assumption that if students have something to say they will find a way to say it. In class, they discuss the implications of what they read. They then write. In these courses, improvement in writing depends mainly on comments and conferences. Student writing is not often discussed in class, although in recent years more and more instructors have found it helpful to devote at least one day a week formally to topics that relate speci-fically to student writing. The reading/writing courses tend to attract students who are already proficient in basic matters of composition. The major task is to help them develop a more mature, identifiable prose style of their own. The readings in these courses are a challenge both to their thinking and to their capacities for expression.

The reading/writing courses are of two varieties. The first is called "Writing about Literature" (English 111); it is a fairly standard offering, designed not specifically as an introduction to genres but as a course that will help students understand the nature of imaginative literature and its ways of creating effects. The writing tends to be interpretive and critical in emphasis. Students learn how to distinguish among summary, interpretation, analysis, and evaluation and how to employ each of these in writing about literary works.

English 111 has not been as popular as two other courses, English 121 and 122, both of which are listed as "Writing about Issues, Topics, and Modes." These are courses about ideas of current and often perennial concern. The readings develop a single theme. Although both the class sessions and the writing thrive to a great extent on controversy and exchange of views, the courses also give instructors and students an opportunity to examine the nature of responsible opinion. The writing tends to be primarily argumentative and persuasive. As in English 111, the time given to the discussion of writing in class may be minimal, but comments and conferences aid students in developing their skill as writers.

The most popular and enduring of the topics we have offered in 121 is one that began in 1970 with the title "Man's Revolutionary Spirit." At that time, revolution was what we saw when we looked out over the campus from our offices. In class, we were reading and talking about Kunen's *The Strawberry Statement*, Cleaver's *Soul on Ice*, and Castaneda's *The Teachings of Don Juan*, as well as works like Malraux's *Man's Fate* and Weiss's *Marat/Sade*. Concurrently, we were offering in 122 a topic entitled "I-Thou: Dimensions of Responsibility," with readings in Camus, Thoreau, Ellison, and Ibsen. Needless to say, in 1970–71, "Dimensions of Responsibility" met an untimely demise.

In 1977, we began to offer "Man's Revolutionary Spirit" in a somewhat different guise. Feminism and the change of social climate have now prompted us to call it "Quests for the Self: Writing about Liberation." The reading list is considerably altered. The political and social emphasis has diminished; the humanistic predominates. The course now concerns the unquenchable rebelliousness of the human spirit, a kind of Faustian theme.

These topics are only representative of others that have come and gone. The flexible and evolving character of the courses has permitted us to be as current as we choose to be, although we have always determined to keep the courses substantive by choosing readings that are intellectually challenging. English 121 and 122 have been our most successful reading/writing courses, but they have not been able to compete in numbers with the straight writing courses, English 171 and 172. English 171 especially tends to attract large numbers of students from lower campus—actually a topographical description of the area, but one that those in the arts and humanities like to think of symbolically. Lower-campus students are those in the sciences and professional schools. They are highly practical-minded. The direct approach of 171 appeals to them.

Besides the strong reading emphasis in English 111, 121, and 122 (I am reminded of E. D. Hirsch's statement at the CCCC meeting in Kansas City: "You cannot possibly write better than you can read"), those courses tend to emphasize writing as a product; that is, instructors focus their attention primarily upon the structure and style of finished pieces of writing submitted by students. By contrast, our second block of courses focuses upon writing as process. As pedagogical theory, this emphasis is newer. It is also sounder for many students in the sense that it gets at the heart of the difficulties they have with inhibitions, apprehensions about correctness, a continuing sense of failure, a reluctance to make a commitment on paper, and seeking in vain for rules and prescriptions that will solve their problems. As a measure to remove the threat of failure and allow for openness and experimentation, English 171 and 172 employ a *Credit/No Credit* system of evaluation. By university standards, *Credit* represents the equivalent of 2.0 or *C* work. *Credit/No Credit* is especially significant in a writing course, because students can learn of their progress, not by seeing *C+* change to *B−*, basically a meaningless gradation, but by assessing the instructor's comments. An instructor assumes the role of reader/critic, not teacher/grader. That shift also characteristically alters the nature of the comments. They are not just justifications of grades; they are remarks designed to encourage and help individual students. Some students flounder under the *Credit/No Credit* arrangement because they are completely grade-conditioned. They need the pressure of grades to work. On the other hand, other students thrive, doing their best work because they are relieved of the pressure of grades. For the former group, we have now created English 181, a course equivalent to 171 in emphasis, but graded in the traditional manner.

English 171 is titled "College Writing: Expository Prose." The concerns of the course are based on the assumption that writing is a form of behavior. Instructors must therefore be concerned with the psychology of the total act from beginning to end. Writing is not simply words on paper—the final product. Writing is overcoming inhibitions. Writing is getting started. Writing is opening up. Writing is controlling. Writing is matching words to thoughts. Writing is feeling as well as thinking. What may be finally transcribed with order and effect is only a selected and edited version of the total process.

Teaching in these sections becomes a way of eliciting the most desirable behavior from each individual as a writer. Class sessions include a series of related and meaningful exercises, not the kind we are familiar with in workbooks, but ones that are designed to create an awareness of the principles of composition by having students discover on their own what is involved. Discovery leads to awareness and thus to a realization that the resources of a good writer are within the grasp of students who will work to acquire them.

The emphasis in English 172 on the research paper was brought about by student demand. When English 172 was first offered, it was conceived somewhat vaguely as an extension of English 171. Students were ready to fill this lack of specific focus by proposing that the course concern itself with the process of writing a sustained paper based on library sources. As a consequence, English 172 now meets a practical need of those students who want instruction in writing a research paper.

The third block of courses, English 104, 105, and 106, is a series of special courses for students not regularly admissible to the university. English 104 and 105 are required; 106 is optional. Educational Opportunity Program students are not automatically placed in 104. They are first examined in reading and writing. If they do well, they are given all of the options that a regularly admissible student has.

In designing EOP classes, we attempted with as much deliberateness as possible not to use labels like *subcollegiate*, *basic*, and *remedial*. English 104 and 105 are called "Introductory Composition"; 106 is called "Practical Forms of Writing." To some people, our insistence that these are not remedial is merely quibbling. But something is not a quibble if it makes a significant difference, and we have found that the descriptive terms we use do make a difference in the attitudes of both instructors and students. *Remedial* is an unfortunate metaphor for a student because it implies a sickness of some kind. What most EOP students need is the opportunity for further growth and development. They are by no means infirm.

English 104 and 105 are hyphenated courses. Hyphenation means that students do not get a grade until they have completed the sequence. Those who begin slowly therefore have a longer time to adjust and develop. We think of 104 and 105 as a ten-hour sequence equivalent to English 171, a three-hour course. In brief, we try to accomplish the objectives of English 171 by the end of 105. We therefore spend a longer time doing comparable work. The intention alone is enough to bolster the spirits of these students, who too often have been given only a new opportunity to fail rather than succeed. The work of the department is supported by a reading/study skills center and a tutoring center. EOP students are given various opportunities to make academic progress.

English 172 and English 106 are the courses among our offerings that have a service function. They are optional. Those who need and want them take them. Otherwise, all of the other courses are designed to improve general writing ability. Under the present requirements for graduation in Arts and Sciences, all of the writing courses may under certain circumstances be used to fulfill a humanities distribution requirement. As a department, we have tried always to think beyond the concept of writing as a basic skill to writing as a mode that allows individuals to gain a sense of self-sufficency and to know fulfillment through self-expression, effective communication, and rational discourse. Our former remedial course, English N-50, was phased out after the summer of 1968, at which time one section drew six students. Because of more selective entrance requirements to the university and an accompanying self-selection, we have not had to make special provisions for unprepared students among those who are regularly admissible.

From this description, it should be clear that the freshman program at the University of Washington is predicated upon diversity. Students do not all learn alike. They need choices, particularly since learning to develop as a writer seems to depend upon finding a way suitable to one's own temperament and most characteristic way of thinking and acting. Before registration, students are given course descriptions and reading lists. Unless they are simply determined to have a 9:30 class whatever it may be, most students seem to find what they want. Student response to our program has been enthusiastic. The contraints upon our offerings have been budgetary. At times we have turned away as many as 200 to 250 students per quarter who want to take courses. After several years of offering from eighty to ninety-five sections, we are again in the fall of 1977 offering 105 sections.

We, like all other colleges, are now feeling the effects of the current exposé of illiteracy that occurs in the press with varying degrees of intensity about every decade. College committees in our school are now considering freshman screening tests and junior proficiency examinations. The truth that is apparent to almost anyone who has taught English more than ten years is that freshman students, despite some variances in their national test scores, do not write remarkably differently in 1977 from the way they did in 1967, 1957, or 1947. Upon occasion, the nation gets conscience-stricken about its general lack of respect for the language. Then the cry for the basics is heard again. It seems only realistic—hardly cynical—to say that illiteracy will be with us always in some proportion, even among the educated.

After years of experience with two essentially different approaches to writing (in the name of jargon, characterize them as product-centered and process-centered), there is little point in trying to assess which is better. Both help students become better writers, but we should quickly note that success with students is more dependent upon a good working relation between teacher and student than upon any structure, syllabus, or textbook. We are therefore concerned about the training of those who teach in the program, whatever the course may be. At present, all courses are taught either by graduate teaching assistants or by acting instructors who have earned their degrees at this university and have taught previously as assistants. Eventually, we try to give each person experience in teaching several different courses, but all new, inexperienced TAs start with 171. There they learn the nuts and bolts of teaching composition. With that background, they know what to do when they are assigned a writing course with supplementary reading material. Without it, they tend to teach only the literature and neglect the composition.

All new teaching assistants, approximately twenty-five each fall, are supervised during their first year, whether or not they have had previous teaching experience. Their orientation begins with three days of intensive study, listening, and discussing before the beginning of classes. The three days, consisting of six different sessions, are divided between formal instruction by the director and small group sessions, for which TAs have been given assignments to prepare. Typically, these concern attitudes, theme assignments, comments, grading, and teaching techniques. The sessions conclude with small groups videotaping their own discussion and then viewing the results. Each TA is also given a student theme to grade and respond to as if it were a first theme. These are reviewed by the director's assistants and commented on chiefly in terms of the tone of the remarks. TAs have this personal response to their work before they ever read their first set of student papers. Later in the quarter, when students have submitted their second essay and it has been read and evaluated by the instructor, revised by the student, and returned, the director's assistants review a large sampling of themes and write an extended critique of the instructor's work in terms of specific papers. This careful examination of the way instructors respond to student work is one of the most important parts of the orientation program. If an instructor's work is highly unsatisfactory, the review is repeated.

Since each teaching assistant is independently and fully responsible for one section of freshman English, each person is required during the fall quarter to follow a supplementary syllabus, written by the director and distributed on a weekly basis. The syllabus includes some review of theoretical material and current research, possible approaches and techniques for the classroom, and suggested theme topics. The syllabuses are not intended to be prescriptive. We are not interested in having everyone turning to page 130 of the rhetoric handbook at the same time on a particular Wednesday. The syllabuses offer choices. TAs learn to organize their own courses within the limits of the general plan suggested by the syllabuses.

During the second quarter, when almost everyone is assigned the same course he taught first quarter, TAs are encouraged to make adjustments in the order of the topics, to eliminate their failures, and to repeat their successes. In a private conference during spring quarter, the director and the assistant then review the kinds of changes that were made and the reasons for them. Together, they discuss and interpret a survey of student opinion that was taken at the end of winter quarter, and in general they reflect upon the year's teaching experience. After the first year, assistants regularly submit student surveys of their teaching to the Freshman English Office. Supervision is informal. One of the important things assistants know is that students do not sign up for elective courses that are poorly taught. The number of freshman English sections and their own jobs are dependent upon a good program and responsible teaching. Fortunately, freshman English continues to do well. Credit must go to our young assistants, whose representatives on the Freshman English Committee help plan the courses and select the texts and who as a group teach the classes conscientiously and enthusiastically. They have kept the freshman English program attractive and helpful.

The Rhetoric Program at the University of Iowa

Cleo Martin, Writing Supervisor, Rhetoric Program

Department responsible for the composition program   Rhetoric Program
Full-time faculty in the program   10
Enrollment policies
    Maximum Enrollment   24
    Minimum Enrollment   12
    Average Enrollment   21
Staffing
    Percentage of freshman rhetoric courses taught by graduate students   90
    Percentage taught by assistant, associate, or full professors   10
Program size
    Number of students enrolled in the rhetoric program in the fall term of 1976   3,000
    Number of sections of freshman rhetoric offered in the fall term of 1976   160
    Number of sections at all levels—literature, composition, film, graduate, undergraduate, etc.—offered by the program in the fall term of 1976   160

Introduction: Unity and Diversity

When I explain to people that my job involves teaching freshman rhetoric at the University of Iowa and directing the Professional Development Program for rhetoric TAs, I nearly always get one of several kinds of responses. Some people ask for more information: "What's rhetoric and what's a TA?" Other people come back with a monosyllabic "Oh," subtly implying, perhaps, that my work would be more interesting to talk about if I were a medieval scholar or a basketball coach or a real-estate agent. Two other kinds of comments about my work are clearly contradictory: (1) "If you've seen one freshman program, you've seen them all." (2) "The extreme diversity within any one program, and from one program to another, suggests that 'you people' have found few principles to unify your efforts; in any case, from what I see and hear, you apparently aren't doing a very good job."

I have come to expect such responses, and they can perhaps guide me—or at least hover in the background in an unsettling way—as I try to describe the rhetoric program. For readers who seek information, I shall try to explain how our program operates. During that explanation, I shall necessarily speak often of the diversity within the program, but there is unity in it, too—unity based on the fact that all rhetoric teachers share some important assumptions with other educators whose professional preoccupation is helping students to improve as communicators.

My discussion as a whole will suggest, I think, that we are at once proud of the rhetoric program and keenly aware of its shortcomings.

The Rhetoric Program and the University

The rhetoric program is an independently funded and administered academic unit of the University of Iowa, directly responsible to the Dean of the College of Liberal Arts and to the College's Educational Policy Committee. Rhetoric courses combine instruction in writing, speaking, reading, and listening, and the courses serve all colleges in the university. Entering students, liberal arts and preprofessional alike, must enroll in rhetoric and remain enrolled until they have met the rhetoric requirement. (The requirement can be met in several ways, as I shall explain later.)

Our teaching staff is composed of some eighty teaching assistants and ten regular faculty members, including the Program Coordinator, the Speech Supervisor, and the Writing Supervisor. All teachers are fully responsible for their own classes, and TAs are "assistants" only in the sense that they teach part time while working toward advanced degrees.

The English and Speech departments are informal affiliates with rhetoric in that they recommend graduate students for appointments as TAs, but rhetoric program administrators are responsible for all staff appointments, for staff training, and for program policy.

Diversity as Related to Rhetoric Program Assumptions

I want to talk now about several aspects of diversity in our program, because diversity is a condition we not only expect but also value. We strongly believe that no group of freshmen, or teachers of freshmen, should be forced to proceed lockstep through a series of predetermined, prescribed activities. From our view, regimentation of any kind is both undesirable and impossible. Recognition of a wide range of individual interests and abilities is the cornerstone of our program, if indeed it has a single cornerstone.

One specific source of diversity is the simple fact that rhetoric courses combine instruction in writing, speaking, reading, and listening. Our teachers, therefore, are drawn from several academic disciplines. As I have said, eighty of our ninety teachers are graduate students, working on advanced degrees in English or speech. Their academic specialties include such diverse areas as comparative literature, fiction writing, communication research, Afro-American literature, drama, public address, eighteenth-century British literature, rhetoric and composition, film, poetry writing, modern American literature, and many others. The ten of us designated as regular faculty have also been trained in various academic areas, and most of us have split appointments in rhetoric and English or rhetoric and speech. Although all teachers have a professional interest in communication (to use that term in its broadest sense), each teacher brings to the program a unique set of abilities and interests. It is more than safe to say that no two of us teach rhetoric in exactly the same way.

Students, of course, come to the program with a wide range of abilities and interests too. Beyond the simple fact that nearly all students have graduated in the upper half of their high-school classes, few generalizations apply. Students come from Iowa farms and from large urban areas; from Nigeria and from Germany; from top-notch high schools and from third-rate high schools. Some entering students have written scarcely a page, while others have written frequently and well; some have won honors in public speaking, while others pale at the thought of talking to more than one person at a time. Any class of twenty students is likely to include a future doctor, engineer, English teacher, professional athlete, and social worker—to name only a few possibilities. The obvious diversity in the student population is a fact we try always to keep in mind. Meeting individual needs is a constant concern. Recognizing that the heterogeneity provides an excellent lay audience for student speakers and writers is always an important consideration as we plan our courses.

Because of wide variation in student ability, we make rather elaborate, early attempts to place students where they seem to belong. In other words, some diversity exists even in the nature of the rhetoric requirement. Although all students must enroll in rhetoric during their first semester, we require no specific number of hours in the program. Some students exempt themselves completely by taking examinations during the first week of the term, while others spend as many as five semesters in our courses or labs.

The program makes two other assumptions that are relevant to the diversity I have been talking about. (1) We assume that rhetoric must be a "performance" course. We believe that students become better communicators by *communicating*, and by receiving criticism from other people. There is no place in our program for underlining nouns and verbs, or for performing exercises that have a dubious relationship to the communication process. (2) We assume that people cannot write or speak well about subjects they neither know about nor care about. These two assumptions dictate a course whose subject matter is largely dictated by the interests of class members. In any one class, students may discuss—orally and in writing—such diverse subjects as the early history of football, the professional requirements for nurses, a current international dispute, and the relative merits of Republicans and Democrats.

Since rhetoric courses also try to provide frequent opportunities for group interaction and exchange of ideas, each class differs from all others, depending upon the views represented in the group. When teachers new to the program ask, "What shall I have students write and speak about?" the usual answer is, "You'll know that when you know the students."

Another rhetoric program assumption is that two principal purposes should direct our work. Part of our effort goes toward preparing students for other courses and for communicating in some future business or professional context—a function of rhetoric courses sometimes called "utilitarian." Yet most rhetoric teachers are unwilling to embrace the you-will-need-this-some-day approach as the sole justification for our courses. We believe that communication experiences in rhetoric should be valuable in and of themselves, here and now, as a part of a student's liberal education—as important, at least, as world history or Golf I. Perhaps an example will clarify my point. We ask that rhetoric students learn to use the university library because they may need to know how to do that for other courses. But another reason for getting students into a library is to have them experience the intellectual pleasure of exploring a subject they care about while working confidently and efficiently in a large library. The insistence upon a dual purpose for rhetoric classes, then, adds dimensions our work would not have if we considered rhetoric strictly a service department.

Finally, the rhetoric program has, for many years, encouraged experimentation with various approaches and methods. Such encouragement clearly increases the diversity in the program, but it reflects the recognition that we have not yet found a perfect way to help students improve as communicators.

Against this background of sometimes confusing, but nearly always productive diversity, I shall try to describe the basic operations of the rhetoric program. I hope that I have already implied a measure of unity in the program by talking about some of our common assumptions. I trust that further evidence of a united effort will become apparent as my account continues.

The Integrated Nature of Rhetoric Courses

For nearly thirty years, all rhetoric courses have combined instruction in reading, writing, speaking, and listening. This structure has been retained because it seems to have some advantages over separate writing and speech courses as they exist in many schools.

The integrated course seems to ensure careful attention to the total communication process. As students improve their abilities to express themselves orally and in writing, they also have experience in analyzing the communications of other speakers and writers. We believe that the ability to listen and read critically and carefully is as crucial in a student's total educational experience as the ability to speak and write effectively. Furthermore, the integrated course seems to foster the active exchange of ideas. When students write and speak to and for one another, an audience develops that is more real than when all writing is directed primarily to the teacher.

Placement of Students

The rhetoric program has developed a rather elaborate placement program. Initial screening is done on the basis of ACT scores in English and Social Science Reading. The admissions office assigns a student either to 10:1 and 10:2 (a two-semester sequence carrying 8 semester hours of credit) or to 10:3 (an accelerated one-semester course carrying 4 semester hours of credit). Ordinarily, about half of the entering freshmen enroll initially in 10:1 and half in 10:3. Because we recognize the obvious fact that machine-scored tests cannot accurately assess students' abilities to communicate, we continue placement efforts during the first week of 10:1 and 10:3 courses.

Early in 10:1, students write two papers and do a diagnostic reading assignment. On the basis of these performances, instructors usually find a few students who communicate well enough to move to 10:3. In addition, the 10:1 placement activities reveal that some students need individual help in addition to class work. Those students are advised to enroll as volunteers for no credit in the reading lab and/or the writing lab. Students who have unusually severe problems in writing or reading may be advised to drop 10:1 and enroll for 10:8 and/or 10:9 (courses that provide individual instruction in reading and writing) before attempting the 10:1–10:2 sequence. After placement activities, the majority of 10:1 students remain in 10:1 and complete the rhetoric requirement in two semesters.

If initially assigned to 10:3, students may attempt exemption examinations, which consist of writing a 450-word essay and giving a four-minute speech. Student work is evaluated independently by two rhetoric instructors, using a departmental rating blank. After the examinations, some students are completely exempt from rhetoric and some are held for only two hours of speech or writing. The majority of 10:3 students remain in 10:3 and complete the rhetoric requirement in one semester.

These procedures probably sound a little more complicated than they actually are. The point is that a student may take a variable number of hours in rhetoric, ranging from zero upward, though only eight hours can be applied toward graduation. A few students continue to work voluntarily in the reading or writing lab throughout most of their academic careers. The placement procedures exist because some students have severe communication problems and others communicate very well when they arrive at the university.

Course Goals and Expectations

Some further placement of students is done throughout the semester, especially the recommending of students for lab work, but most students are located in courses by the second week of the semester. At that point, all rhetoric courses have some common general goals as set forth in the *Rhetoric Faculty Handbook*:

While the entire College of Liberal Arts program should help students evaluate their experience and anticipate the possibilities in their present and future lives, the Rhetoric Program offers direct experience in exploring, formulating, and evaluating these possibilities through oral and written communication.

Students are expected to increase their ability to investigate, analyze, evaluate and respond to the ideas, beliefs, and attitudes of other writers and speakers and to use responsibly various resources of information and ideas. But the main focus in the classroom is on the students' own communication; the primary responsibility of the course is to help students clarify their own thinking and improve their communication with others.

The primary assumption implicit in these goals is the centrality of speaking, writing, listening, and reading activities in all rhetoric courses. The students in all classes are exposed to a wide variety of attitudes, ideas, and information through active verbal exchange. Students develop their abilities to communicate through expressing their ideas to the group, both orally and in writing. They develop ways to express ideas more effectively through careful consideration of the reactions and suggestions of other students and the teacher. They expand their ideas through extensive reading of and careful listening to the ideas of others.

Rhetoric teachers, therefore, are asked to keep the focus of the course on student communication, to create a learning atmosphere conducive to student participation, to provide suggestions for each student communicator. We remind teachers that an assignment or activity is valuable only insofar as it relates to the improvement of students' communication abilities, and we point out that there should be little lecturing by the teachers of rhetoric courses.

In summary, the instruction in rhetoric courses focuses on activities designed to help students become more competent and effective communicators. Specifically, we ask that these activities include, for each student, writing at least ten essays, doing eight critical-reading assignments, and giving at least five oral presentations each semester.

Course Content

The *Course Manual for Teachers* provides a general outline for the 10:1–10:2 sequence and for the 10:3 accelerated course under seven unit headings: (1) "Creating a Context for Informal Interpersonal Communication," (2) "Sequencing Material for a Familiar Audience," (3) "Developing Complex Messages for an Analytical Audience," (4) "Refining Judgmental Skills in Assessing and Responding to Rhetorical Situations," (5) "Analyzing and Supporting Value Judgments for Audiences with Divergent Viewpoints," (6) "Analyzing and Supporting Arguments for Audiences with Divergent Viewpoints," (7) "Applying Rhetorical Principles in Specialized Academic Situations."

The *Manual* outline develops each of these general headings in some detail, suggesting that the audience role of the teacher and the class changes as the content of the writing, speaking, and reading changes and as the emphasis upon various rhetorical principles changes. Teachers meet frequently to exchange specific methods, assignments, and suggestions for implementing the course outline.

During roughly the first half of 10:1 and the first fourth of 10:3, students are encouraged to talk and write about their direct personal experience, their own areas of interest and knowledge. By this means, the group develops into a familiar audience for oral and written activities. As the course moves along, the exchange of ideas in class and the course emphasis on reading should help students broaden their perspectives and develop the ability to write or speak to almost any audience about subjects previously unfamiliar to the writer or speaker.

By the end of 10:1–10:2 or 10:3, students should have had experience and instruction in locating, evaluating, and communicating information that reflects a variety of viewpoints; focusing and restricting the central idea of a communication; making clear the purpose or thesis of a communication; supporting generalizations with specific material or evidence from their own experience and from reading; and developing a logical sequence of subordinate ideas, reasons, steps, or issues. Students should also have received practice and instruction in the use of the library and in research procedures. By the end of a rhetoric course, the language in student essays and speeches should be direct, concise, vivid, and purposeful. Writers should be able to use standard English, and speakers should exhibit control over the techniques of oral delivery sufficient to engage and hold the attention of a group.

Evaluation of Student Work:
The Reader-Listener Response Blank

An analytical response blank is used throughout the rhetoric program for instruction and for evaluation of student work. All instructors are asked to become familiar with it, to recognize its value and limitations, and to use their own judgment about how extensively they use it in their classes. The blank is composed of five categories, or criteria: Content, Organization, Expression, Delivery (for speeches), and Mechanics (for papers). The categories are described briefly on the blank itself, and the *Course Manual* describes them in some detail.

The limitations of the blank are obvious. A speech or essay is an organic whole that suffers if dissected, and certainly no set of categories can describe accurately the variety of forms excellent oral and written communication can take. However, most rhetoric instructors find some benefit in using the blank, at least on occasion, and there are some times when all instructors are asked to use it.

In the interest of fairness to students, all instructors are required to use the blank in rating exemption examinations. The categories should help students understand the criteria for exemption, and help teachers apply the criteria with reasonable consistency. Furthermore, all instructors are asked to familiarize their students with the blank because it suggests the rhetoric program's minimal expectations for student work.

The extent to which the blank is used in classroom situations and the nature of its use vary widely from one instructor to another. Some instructors use it as a shorthand method of commenting, although the blank can in no way substitute for careful annotation of papers. Other instructors use the categories on the blank primarily to show students areas of strength and weakness in their speaking and writing. Still other instructors use the blank as a helpful way of assigning letter grades to individual speeches or papers.

Evaluation of Student Work:
The University of Iowa Grading System

Since anybody who has ever worked with student writers and speakers is aware of the difficulties involved in grading, I will not belabor that subject. Most of us feel qualified for the evaluator-role in one sense—pointing out strengths and weaknesses in student work and making suggestions for improvement. The difficulty comes when we must assess each student's work in terms of a final letter grade.

The Educational Policy Committee has spent much time in recent years discussing alternatives to the *A-B-C-D-F* grading system, but they have found no plan satisfactory to the majority of the faculty. Therefore, the rhetoric program, like all other divisions of the college, uses the five-point scale when assigning final grades. Each instructor is free to devise his or her own methods for arriving at a student's final grade. Two student options do mitigate the grading problem: Rhetoric can be taken on a *Pass/Fail* basis. And any course can be repeated under a Second-Grade Option plan, thereby erasing the earlier grade.

Staff Training: The Rhetoric Professional Development Program

The rhetoric Professional Development Program (PDP) for teachers exists primarily for the purpose of providing teachers with regular opportunities to exchange ideas and information and to discuss teaching theories and techniques. PDP is so named because its assumptions are somewhat different from those of programs in other schools, usually called "staff training" programs. To be sure, one PDP purpose is to orient new teachers to the rhetoric program, but we also assume that new teachers bring with them a rich supply of ideas that can be helpful to all of us. We assume that teachers continue to "develop professionally" throughout their careers, and regular exchange of views with colleagues can help toward that end.

One PDP project is a two-day, preregistration workshop, which acquaints new teachers with the rhetoric program and acquaints all members of the staff with one another. Throughout the semester, PDP meets weekly on Thursdays from 3:30 to 5:20 P.M., a period all instructors are asked to keep free. The sessions vary in format, including some small group sessions, some individual or group presentations to the whole staff, and some individual conferences.

PDP is organized by a committee of experienced TAs and regular faculty members. Committee members plan, advertise, and participate in the weekly sessions, confer with new instructors, locate and advertise teaching resources, and seek out teachers who can make special contributions to PDP sessions.

Program Strengths and Problems: A Summary

The diversities I discussed early in this selection are, perhaps, the basis for our program's greatest strengths, and the source of some of our most troublesome problems. If our teachers and students were all timid little persons of like mind, and if we could devise the proper hurdles for all students to jump over on their way to effective communication, then our days would be more serene. But then, of course, our program would not deserve to exist. There is no doubt that the presence of teachers with a variety of academic backgrounds and teaching philosophies lends an exciting vitality to our program. We learn from each other, and we are all the better for that. The wide range of student abilities in any one class is a persistent problem, but I can only applaud the strong dedication of our staff to the belief that we must do everything we can to meet the communication needs of each individual student. Two other major concerns are perennially present: Most of us feel some sense of inadequacy in giving students the instruction they deserve in all four areas of the course—reading, writing, speaking, and listening. Second, we are concerned that requirements and standards may be uneven from one section to another. The Rhetoric Professional Development Program, now in its fourth year, appears, however, to be making some progress toward solving the most urgent problems.

The Freshman Writing Program at the University of Southern California

Sylvia Manning, Chairman of the Freshman Writing Program

Department responsible for the composition program   Freshman Writing Program
Full-time faculty in the program   1
Enrollment policies
     Maximum Enrollment   25
     Minimum Enrollment   15
     Average Enrollment   22–23
Staffing
     Percentage of freshman composition courses taught by graduate students   95
     Percentage taught by assistant, associate, and/or full professors   5
Program size
     Number of students enrolled in the freshman composition program in the fall term of 1976   2,835
     Number of sections of freshman composition offered by *all* departments in the fall term of 1976   130
     Number of sections offered by the English department in the fall term of 1976   113
     Number of sections at all levels—literature, composition, film, graduate, undergraduate, etc.—offered by the English department in the fall term of 1976   200

The College of Letters, Arts, and Sciences at the University of Southern California has for decades required two semesters of writing for all Bachelor of Arts degrees. Until 1963 the requirement was simply stated: English *ab*. In 1963–64 there began a process of modification that after fifteen years will have come full spiral. Starting in 1963–64 students could substitute some half-dozen courses for the English *b* requirement, courses such as logic (in philosophy) and spoken communication (in speech). By 1968–69, they could go to comparative literature for the equivalent of English *a*, by 1972–73 to comparative literature or classics, by 1973–74 to Slavic or to cinema if they were cinema majors, and by 1974–75 to linguistics. Through 1977–78 the breadth of choice continued: six courses for the *a* requirement and twelve courses for the *b* requirement. The 1978–79 catalog again has a simply stated writing requirement: Composition 101, offered by the freshman writing program.

The writing requirement had become diffuse, unknowable, and finally too much a bone of interdepartmental contention. The freshman writing program will be large (the only absolutely required course for about 2,500 freshmen each year, for two semesters) but free of competing interests because it will be a separate unit within the university, not merely part of a department that has multiple responsibilities. Its creation reflects the recent popular concern with student writing, but it will not merely go back—or even forward—to basics.

Composition 101 will be taught almost entirely by graduate students, hired primarily from the departments whose TAs have taught the 101 courses in the past (English, comparative literature, linguistics, and the rest) but theoretically from any department that can present qualified students. We may also hire regular faculty members from various departments to teach in the program, but the writing program itself will never hire an independent faculty who do not have student or faculty appointments elsewhere at USC. We want to separate the program administratively from other units in the college, but not conceptually. Though our revised general education requirements will probably speak of the writing requirement as a "skill requirement," and though our structure will make the course what is often called a "proficiency requirement," we believe that our program is neither "skill" nor "service" but the core of whatever liberal and liberating education students receive at this institution.[1]

And if we fail in that more glorious definition, there is something else our course certainly will be: the single experience undergone by all freshmen at USC. If only for our potential influence upon the college's attrition rate, we have great cause to make that experience a good one. We work, therefore, from certain pedagogical principles now commonplace. One is that this first experience should not be one of failure, prediction of failure, or social or intellectual stigma. Another is that students learn at different rates. A third is that there is almost infinite individual variation in students' difficulties with writing. A fourth is that writing is something more fundamental than the niceties of edited standard English, and a fifth that teachers of writing are made, not born.

Our first three principles are reflected in the structure of the course that satisfies the writing requirement. Composition 101 is an eight-unit course that we expect most students will take two semesters to complete. Some students will take only one semester, some will take three, some will take none, but no one will begin a career at USC by being remanded into a "remedial" or "basic" course. All students will enroll in Composition 101, a year-long course. A few, whose high-school English grades and verbal SAT scores are very high, will be offered the opportunity to test out of the course at the very start. They will achieve a grade of *A* on the test, and be awarded eight units of *A* credit, or they will continue in the course. At the end of the first semester, interim grades will be awarded to all students, but only grades of *A* or *In Progress*. Those with grades of *A* will not be required to continue attendance in the course. At the end of the second semester, grades of *A, B, C, D,* or *In Progress* will be awarded. Those who receive grades of *In Progress* will continue in the course for a third semester, though they will neither receive extra credit nor pay extra tuition for it. At the end of the third semester, it will be possible to receive a grade of *A, B, C, D,* or *F*. At that point the course will fall under the general college regulation that allows students who have failed a course to repeat the course and receive the average of their two grades. Students repeating Composition 101 will have another three semesters available to them.

In any section of Composition 101, not only will the students be untracked, but there will be students in their first, second, and third semester of the course. Is it possible to teach a class of this sort? We think it is—at least as possible as to teach a supposedly more homogeneous class—if the instructors are properly trained. We have called the course "Freshman Writing Workshop" to indicate its internal heterogeneity. Its pedagogy will be familiar to those who remember the "Keller method" or "PSI classroom," and will be obvious to anyone who thinks about a class in painting or ceramics. Art studio classes have always been workshops, because no one ever expected people to paint or fashion clay in tandem. There will be lectures in our writing workshops, but most of the time the classroom will look quite disorderly, with students working alone or in small groups and the instructor moving among them. Some students may at times tutor other students, but mostly the peer groups will be just that: students will write to communicate and with each other will test their writing as communication and discuss its problems.

The workshop structure and the absence of remedial classes will both depend upon the assistance of our writing laboratory. Students will come to the laboratory mostly by referral from their composition instructors, and usually with a specific recommendation. The difficulties of motivation that writing labs almost always encounter we hope to alleviate by a procedure that will then tie the students' assignments in the lab directly to their writing workshops, so that the work in the lab is clearly related to the work in the course. Through the lab those students who need more time and attention than even three semesters in the workshops can provide will get it.

The lab has another important role: it enables us to live by our fourth principle, that writing is something more fundamental than the niceties of standard English. Because of the lab and its tutorials, programed texts, and computer programs, we can attend to matters such as punctuation, spelling, grammar, and so forth without making them central to the course in writing. Our instructors are thereby freed to deal with more fundamental and interesting matters of style, such as syntactic fluency, invention, problem solving, and conceptualization. We can avoid to a great extent the debilitation that comes when a class in writing becomes a class in the conventions of the accepted written dialect, and we can concentrate instead upon the problems of investing sentences, paragraphs, and essays with meaning.[2]

We do not plan to set texts or syllabuses. We may end up with a list of recommended texts mainly for the purpose of assisting the logistical problems of the bookstore, but otherwise we feel no call for uniformity. We will encourage, as we have in the past, the exchange of student papers among the students and the use in the workshop of papers students are preparing for other classes, because these are two ways to encourage the idea of writing as medium between writer and one or more readers. And we can afford to give up uniformity of process because we will impose a certain uniformity of goal. That is, the course will conclude with a uniform examination. The grades students receive at the end of the semester will be a combination of the grades assigned for their term's work by the instructor and the scores they achieve on the uniform test. We present the test without apology, but with care. It will have two parts, a machine-scored section that we expect to purchase, and an essay section that we will develop ourselves. The essay topics will be pretested in our program, and the essays will be read by our instructors by the "global reading" system. The test will give a certain uniformity of direction to the workshops. We are not concerned with the matter of "teaching to the exam," because the standards of the exam will be fully aligned with the goals of the course. The uniform exam will also provide one kind of evaluation of the workshops, giving us some data from which to test the course itself. At the same time, the limited validity of such testing and the importance of the instructors' authority will be reflected in the due weight given to the term grades assigned directly by the instructors. Finally, the process of reading the exam essays will probably establish standards of essay grading that will carry over to the grading in the workshops.

There is one other force against the total freedom that the lack of set texts or syllabuses might imply. We will teach writing: not literature, not cultural history, but writing. We allow that an excellent course in writing might take as its sole text *Moby-Dick* or *Soul on Ice,* but we will check booklists and will ask questions when such particular interests appear dominant. We will refuse to segregate our classes not only by students' ability but by secondary subject matters. The exception will be the special classes for USC's fairly large population of foreign undergraduates, who are significantly better served, we think, by instructors with a real interest in English as a second language.

We will demand a great deal from our instructors, but we won't expect to have them meet our demands unassisted. For some time USC has given its TAs a training course in rhetorical theory that runs through their first semester's teaching assignment. This credit-bearing course has been accompanied by the less formal coaching of new instructors by those more experienced (the assignment of 5 "supervisees" constitutes the equivalent, for a supervising TA, of teaching one section). The new training course we envision will be an intensive course (40 hours per week) that will take place just before the opening of each fall term. The first part of the course will combine rhetorical theory and applied linguistics. Much of it will be the same as what the present course covers: the composing process (Emig's *The Composing Process of Twelfth Graders, Writers at Work*); contemporary stylistics; syntactic fluency

(Christensen, Mellon, O'Hare); invention, dialectic, "topics," models and heuristics (Abraham Kaplan, Roman Jakobson, Young, Becker, Pike); form (structuralist theory, Keith Fort's "Form, Authority, and the Critical Essay," W. Ross Winterowd); various concepts from modern linguistics. Toward the end the course will turn to the practical matter of running the kind of workshop we expect, and it will culminate in the students' reading of the first set of uniform essay exams—that by which the best freshman writers may test out of the course at the very start. This major segment of the course will be taught by Ross Winterowd and Robert Kaplan. The practical part will then continue through the fall semester, probably in weekly or biweekly meetings. We have not yet worked out who will conduct those meetings or how, but we hope to retain some of the advantages we have found in the use of senior TAs, namely the development of a confidential rather than evaluative relationship.

A final word of hesitation. At the time of writing, the program I have described does not exist. The composition committee has the goodwill of all interested parties at USC, and a general mandate to create the best program it can devise. But what we have devised will require special forms of many current practices (for instance, there is not yet anything like an undergraduate *In Progress* grade at USC), and between the best-laid plans and the working program may fall many a shadow. Planning is a sort of luxurious state, a kind of innocence we now enjoy. As we look toward experience, our being a program separate from any of the departments strikes me as a possible advantage. It gives us the possibility of failure on a rather grand scale, but it also gives us the possibility of creating an unusually desirable atmosphere around the whole matter of freshman writing. We work against the disadvantage of teaching a required course, for the simple reason that requirements generate resistance. On the other hand, we are teaching not some department's lowest-level course, bread-and-butter course, service or dues-paying course, but the program's *only* course. Our instructors are not the department's lowest-ranking teachers, but its whole ladder. The freshmen are not a means of supporting graduate seminars, but our only students. We have given the administrative assistant who will help launch this program over the next year one major charge: make this program one in which the students and the instructors know that they matter supremely, in which the students may be surprised to find writing good to learn, and in which the instructors are happy to work.

Notes

[1] The language of my last clause is taken from W. Ross Winterowd, whose work is at the conceptual center of our program. The "we" of this essay refers to the chairman of the freshman writing program and her advisory committee: Ross Winterowd; linguist Robert Kaplan; faculty members from English, classics and comparative literature, and business; and a graduate student.

[2] Again, I am using the language of Ross Winterowd. The last two sentences are entirely paraphrased from his unpublished writing.

The Interdepartmental Composition Program at Central College

Barbara Fassler, Chairperson of the Humanities Division

Department responsible for the composition program   Each department certifies
its own majors.
Full-time faculty in the English Department   6
Enrollment policies
Maximum Enrollment   30
Minimum Enrollment   6
Average Enrollment   23
Staffing
All freshman composition courses at Central College are taught by assistant, associate, or full professors.
Program size
Number of students enrolled in the freshman composition program in the fall term of 1976   225
Number of sections of freshman composition offered in the fall term of 1976   7
Number of sections at all levels—literature, composition, film, graduate, undergraduate, etc.—offered by the department in the fall term of 1976   18

For years now English teachers have told themselves that the teaching of writing—and, for that matter, of reading and speaking—cannot be accomplished by the English department alone; on occasion, English teachers have even told their colleagues in other departments and the administrators of their college the same thing. It has done little good. In most colleges nothing has changed. What we needed was an emergency—or, what's just as good, something that our colleagues would perceive as an emergency—to get the entire faculty of a college to commit itself to teaching basic skills. Right now, college administrators and teachers in all disciplines *believe* there is an emergency: students' poor command of reading, writing, and oral communication. Perhaps the time is right to implement a campus-wide skills program. At Central College (a private, four-year liberal arts college of 1,200 students), we have, in fact, developed a basic skills program that involves every department and a substantial percentage of the college's faculty. Quite simply, the college's writing proficiency requirement is as follows: Each major department in the college must certify each of its graduating majors as possessing the basic writing, reading, and oral communication skills necessary to function adequately in that discipline.

There are two steps in developing a basic skills program that involves the entire faculty of an institution: first, the unit that has historically been charged with assuring that students are literate and articulate—usually the English department, of course—must build a strong support system for teaching basic skills. Second, the entire faculty must accept formally the responsibility for teaching basic skills: the commitment includes agreeing to make skills instruction part of *every* course in the college and then accepting the responsibility for certifying the basic skills competence of everyone who graduates from the college.

The Support System

The first step in beginning an institution-wide writing program is to develop a strong support system. A few English department faculty members began to construct our support system five years ago when they opened a noncredit writing lab and initiated a course that trained upperclass students to tutor in the lab. Then they offered an eight-hour, in-service workshop to train faculty from other disciplines to evaluate and develop student writing skills. From those two services has evolved our present support system, now directed by a full-time skills coordinator (a position funded by HEW under "Special Services for Economically Disadvantaged Students") and an elected faculty skills council. In building our program, we have always tried to involve and train a wide variety of faculty, a step that I believe was the basis for our success, two years ago, in getting our faculty to vote for the second aspect of our skills program—formal responsibility.

For students who need special training in basic skills, the support system must offer both a full complement of credit courses in all skills and a drop-in skills lab that provides immediate, free help. The Central College lab, staffed by a faculty director and trained upperclass student tutors, handles writing, reading, and oral communication and also provides subject-area tutors. Faculty in all disciplines are asked to help select the tutors—an important way of keeping all faculty involved in the lab. Many of the subject-area tutors and all of the skills tutors take one of two courses: "Teaching Writing" or "Teaching Reading." All subject-area tutors also attend a three-day workshop, funded by Exxon, to train them to improve students' reading, writing, and study skills no matter what the subject area.

The support system for faculty is perhaps even more important than that for students. More often than not, faculty members who have not been trained to teach composition courses grade on content rather than writing, or they waste their energies stabbing at split infinitives and other villains of their own school days, or they attack a hundred errors of various types and seriousness without helping the student to classify deficiencies and set priorities, or they chop at dialect characteristics in such a way as to wound the student's self-respect unnecessarily, or they allow to pass unchallenged a mechanically correct but mediocre writer who could benefit greatly from some pointers about paragraph coherence, parallelism, or variation of sentence patterns. In short, whether knowingly or unknowingly, they base students' grades partly on facility of oral expression, but they never offer students analyses of their communication styles; they ascribe poor essay test performance to laziness, writing deficiencies, or lack of intelligence, but they fail to recognize and attack the reading comprehension problems that result in poor essays. To remedy these weaknesses and to build faculty expertise and self-confidence, in-service workshops have, for us, been an effective aid. Over the past several years we have offered eight-hour seminars on developing student reading and writing skills in subject-area courses. In addition, this past fall the annual three-day faculty workshop was devoted to helping faculty evaluate and develop student basic skills within subject-area courses. So that workshop leaders can later function as a continuing resource for their colleagues, we have our own faculty—rather than outside consultants—teach these workshops. Later in the term, after an economics professor, for example, has graded a set of essays from his "Principles of Economics" class and used his skills to diagnose writing problems and to give helpful criticism to students, a member of the English faculty can read the papers and give *him* suggestions about his comments to the students.

Besides sponsoring in-service workshops and acting as an ongoing resource, the leaders of the skills program need to be a continuing presence in every faculty person's life and mailbox. We send forms asking teachers to list students they think could benefit from the lab; we ask for teachers' recommendations for possible lab tutors; we ask members of each department for suggestions about how the lab could be more useful to their students. In short, we try to be one of the squeakiest wheels on campus.

As well as directing the labs for students, and offering workshops, guidance, and mailbox-stuffers for faculty, the Skills Council operates a broad system of record-keeping to keep track of every student's development in writing, reading, and oral communication skills. Code numbers in each skills area are assigned to freshmen on the basis of their ACT scores, a written essay, the Nelson-Denny Reading Test, and the student's self-evaluation. By using the students' folders of skills information, which are continuously updated by skills course teachers, lab staff, and advisers, the advisers can counsel students about their academic goals and program; departments can use the folders in evaluating the skills proficiency of their majors; and the lab staff can use the folders in evaluating the needs of drop-ins.

Making the Entire Faculty Responsible for Skills

Thus supported, workshopped, nagged, and supplied with records, faculty should be encouraged to assume formal responsibility for the development of basic skills in their students. There are two ways to define the responsibility of the faculty: one approach makes the faculty members responsible for structuring skills development into their courses; the other makes the faculty as a whole responsible for the skills competence of graduates. The first method provides development for all students in a course regardless of their level of competence; the second ensures that all students reach a certain minimum competence before graduation. Central College travels both roads simultaneously, and so, I believe, can most institutions.

The first approach has been implemented at Central by the Skills Council's asking departments to designate certain courses from their regular curriculum as *skills* courses in writing, reading, oral communication, or any combination of these areas. The council assumes that if twenty-five percent of the college's total course offerings require heavy work in basic skills, most students will float into one or several such courses before graduating. Other institutions may lay their seines differently, but the principle is that one must go beyond general sermons about being fishers and actually plan how to lay out the nets, identifying exactly which courses and teachers are responsible for emphasizing which skills.

To earn its special label, a skills course must fulfill the following conditions: First, the course must include extensive practice and performance of the skill. Second, the teacher must give detailed evaluations of each student's performance in each skill and provide as much actual instruction and help as possible—always, of course, calling upon the labs and faculty resource persons for help. For example, the history teacher might write detailed comments about writing style on student papers, or discuss writing style in individual student conferences, or critique rough drafts as well as final papers. The sociology teacher in a reading skills class might use the CLOZE test to monitor the relationship between the class text and student reading levels, or demonstrate and supervise proper reading of a portion of the text, or, with the help of one of the resource people in reading, structure comprehension exercises based on the class text. In a psychology class that emphasizes oral communication, the student might receive careful analysis of contributions to class discussion or of presentations before the class. Finally, the teacher of any course designated as a skills course must provide a formal evaluation of the skills each student commands by the end of the course. A student may receive a course grade of C, which reflects both content mastery and facility of expression, but the teacher will also assign the student a code number in each skills area. That code is not recorded on the permanent transcript, but it is sent to the skills center, where it becomes part of the student's file and is forwarded to the student's academic adviser.

Since teaching a skills course requires extra effort from the teacher, who, in most cases, must learn new techniques of student evaluation, it is not always easy to find volunteers for such courses. One helpful step is for the educational system to reward skills teachers by making skills courses smaller than regular courses, by providing recognition or reduced loads for skills faculty, or by lending research support to faculty who are developing expertise in the teaching of skills in subject-area courses.

Faculty can perhaps be rewarded for volunteering to teach skills courses, but what makes students elect such courses? Central College's answer to this problem is to refrain from identifying skills courses in any publication handed to students. Advisers have lists that they use to counsel students, but otherwise students are expected to regard skills courses as kin to rainy days—they may spoil the picnic, but they are unavoidable and, after all, they do considerable good. Our goal is to enlist students' understanding and loyalty in what we are trying to do, and to have so many skills courses that students do not regard such courses as unusual.

One could, however, label the skills courses and then perhaps give special recognition on the student's transcript for successful completion of the courses, a mark that could be helpful in applying for employment or graduate school. Finally, one could make one or more skills courses a requirement for graduation or designate them as useful preparation or acceptable substitutes for proficiency requirements.

A second way in which formal responsibility for skills may be shouldered by the entire faculty is to ask the faculty to make sure that students under their care command certain basic communication skills before graduating. An institution may delegate this task to the English department or some other isolated subculture, which may administer a standard test to every student, but Central has chosen to involve all faculty. We delegate this task to the various departments, each of which is responsible for certifying that, before graduation, each of its majors possesses the minimum reading, writing, and oral communication skills necessary to function adequately in that field. With the help of the Skills Council and of experts in the skills areas, each department determines what standards apply for its discipline and how students will demonstrate competence. Interdepartmental discussions make departments aware of what others are doing and encourage some unanimity (or at least discourage wild eccentricity). Published statements by each department inform students what is expected of them. When a student applies for a history major, for example, the department immediately constructs his skills profile, using the initial codes assigned him as a freshman, plus later test scores, evaluations from his teachers, coding from any skills courses he has had, and in some cases a department test. If it appears that the student is deficient in the basic skills needed for that discipline, he is informed in writing and given specific guidelines and goals for remediation. He might be asked to pass a fundamental composition course with a grade of *C* or better; he might work in the oral skills lab until the director can certify that he has reached a certain level of competence; he might have to take a history course in which the professor must make sure that those who pass have demonstrated competence in basic skills necessary to historians. Nearly all deficient students will, in such a system, either be helped toward competence or advised into other fields; during the last semester, refusals of certification are rare. When a department does refuse endorsement, the graduation of that student is not automatically denied; it is thrown open to the action of the elected student-faculty Credits Committee, which decides these and other such cases.

Granted there are plenty of problems in this system, and since it is very new at Central, we have not completely worked out the bugs; our belief, however, is that making departments responsible for certifying the skills proficiency of their majors is an effective way to encourage departments to participate in the institution-wide effort to improve students' skills. We also hope to beat the impersonality, the cultural biases, and the rigidity of standardized tests graded by machines or by strangers. In our program, the student is evaluated by a group of teachers in his own discipline—teachers who have observed his capabilities in various situations over a period of time. We also hope to tap the considerable excitement and motivation students bring to their major field, and to make the basic skills more obviously relevant to them—not by saying, "To graduate from Central you must pass this test or this course," but by saying, "To be a biologist you will need certain kinds of basic skills, and before you can graduate as a biology major, you must show our biology faculty that you possess those skills." Of course, this makes it incumbent upon the biology faculty to know what skills are necessary to biologists, how those skills may be measured, and how they may be developed; and it virtually guarantees that biology teachers will come to the support system for training, resources, suggestions, and information. So the two systems—support and responsibility—intertwine. Though other institutions may clothe them in different colors, the basic principles that have emerged from the program at Central may prove helpful to a wide variety of schools attempting to involve their entire faculties in the effort to improve students' proficiency in reading, writing, and oral communication.

The Undergraduate Composition Program in the Michigan State University English Department

Jay B. Ludwig, Director of Writing Programs

Departments responsible for the composition program
English, American Thought and Language, and two Residential Colleges—James Madison College and Lyman Briggs College

Full-time faculty in the English department   49

Enrollment policies in the English department's courses
Maximum Enrollment   20
Minimum Enrollment   10
Average Enrollment   19

Staffing
Percentage of freshman composition courses offered by the English department taught by instructors or lecturers on full-time appointment   67
Percentage taught by assistant, associate, and/or full professors   33

Program size
Number of students enrolled in freshman composition courses offered by the English department in the fall term of 1976   227
Number of sections of freshman composition offered in the fall term of 1976   12
Number of sections at all levels—literature, composition, film, graduate, undergraduate, etc.—offered by the English department in the fall term of 1976   122

In the Michigan State English department's program, freshman composition itself is a relatively small course. Michigan State's general education program, which has its own separate faculty, and three residential colleges, all of which administer their own writing programs, have the responsibility for providing training in composition to the majority of our freshmen. The English department's freshman writing course, a two-term sequence, enrolls about two hundred students a year, ten sections. All of the students come from the College of Arts and Letters or the Honors College. The department also has a sophomore composition course, a one-term writing workshop. In contrast to our freshman course, the sophomore course averages thirty sections per term and has been in such demand by students whose major departments require it that until recently preference in enrollment has been given to graduating seniors. These two courses, plus a nonfiction prose course that is part of our creative writing sequence and a year-long experimental sequence in scientific writing, constitute the whole undergraduate composition program of the Michigan State English department. Each of the courses I have mentioned has passed well beyond the mix of theme writing, essay anthologies, and exercises that has come to typify freshman composition. All four courses are rich and challenging ones to take or to teach. And they are so because each course is informed by theory and research on language, writing, and writing pedagogy; because each is a close, clear part of an *English* department program; and because our department is concerned to communicate our sense of what we know about the teaching of writing—to be accountable for our program—to our students, to the rest of the faculty at MSU, and to others professionally engaged in the teaching of composition.

The freshman writing course, English 101/102, is relatively new, having been developed in the late sixties. The course was nurtured with extreme care. For three years after its inception, staff members held weekly meetings in which they refined the principles of the course and worked to solve the day-to-day problems they encountered teaching it. Through the ongoing attention the course received, it acquired, and has sustained, a complex identity. Particular versions of the course vary markedly in their details, their style, and their relative adherence to traditional methods; but common characteristics—underlying principles—make each section recognizable as the same course, as a brother or sister to the other sections being taught in any particular year. The principles underlying the course are complicated. They rest on an understanding of the organic form of language, on an awareness of the complexity of communication, and on a belief in the power of language both to shape and to encode thought and feeling. If such a paradox can make sense, a good characterization of English 101/102 would be that it is a "literary" composition course, that is, a course that draws confidently and substantially on ideas about writing, about reading, and about language—ideas that also inform our interest in the study of literature. Our freshman writing course is not cut off from the perspectives and energies the department brings to the teaching of literature. It is distinctly and confidently an English course, though it enrolls students from throughout the university and is specifically designed to be a course in general writing development, not a creative writing course, a literature course, or (merely) a course in the mechanics of writing. The influences —principles, perspectives, theories—that inform the course were, moreover, not only, or even most obviously, literary. The 1966 Dartmouth Seminar influenced the course design, at least in a general way. James Moffett's work contributed both to the basic principles on which the course was built and to the details of how it is taught, and developers of the course drew ideas and principles from a great many more sources. They were at the same time, of course, also paying careful attention to their own experience as students and as teachers of writing.

The underlying principles to which I have been alluding translate into a course that looks very different from the traditional freshman composition course. Though it runs two terms, we consider it one course and make good on that assumption by requiring students to enroll in the same section with the same instructor both terms. This requirement, which causes remarkably few problems, allows our teachers and students the time needed to work seriously on writing development. The fact that students and instructors work together closely for about six months as well as the fact that sections are limited to twenty students and meet four times a week gives us an unusually powerful opportunity to pay attention to each student's writing and to keep paying attention to it until we and our student know how to deal with the writing problems he or she is encountering. In addition, the duration and closeness of contact help our students through their period of adjustment to the university. Each section of 101/102 is a relatively stable place, small and relaxed enough to allow students to get to know each other.

The writing done in the course is itself unusual in that we are striving to help our students develop their general ability as writers at the same time that we take seriously the idea that they should write through the medium of their own personal voice. Several consequences flow from our emphasis on the idea, stated simply, that all writing is personal. Writing assignments stay personal virtually throughout the two terms. We place our students in more complicated writing situations with respect to subject and audience as the course progresses and thereby exercise each student's voice in increasingly "objective" writing situations. Early writing assignments may center on relatively direct explorations of self—exercises in perception, for instance, or attempts at defining present identity. Next, we ask our students to work on explorations of self in particular contexts—for instance, self in a particular geographical setting or, much harder, at a particular moment in the past. These assignments in turn give place to work on self and others, biographical or fictional writing, and from there move to writing in which self and issues must be brought together. Typically and by tradition an extended autobiographical writing has been the culminating assignment of the first term's work. The progressively decentered sequence of assignments, as well as the emphasis on self in each, is designed to help our students learn to handle virtually any writing task in a way that is both technically adept and also in touch with its own sources in the personality and language of its author.

The experience of writing with one's own voice and out of one's own experience is made richer by the fact that our students act as audience and editors for each other. Throughout the two terms the most typical classroom activity of English 101/102 is class discussion of student writing. Virtually all writing assignments done for the course are dittoed for reading by everyone. Discussion formats vary from day to day and class to class: a whole class may be discussing one student's paper, or groups of four may be exchanging papers, or pairs of students may be editing each other's rough drafts. It is our experience that student discussion of papers, particularly over a long time and with the process guided or taught by an instructor, is an invaluable aid to writing and reading development. The class as audience gives each of our students someone to write to. Probably even more important, it provides an interested, sympathetic chorus of response to each student's effort to communicate in written language. Students can be impressive writing teachers, editors, and sympathizers. And so they benefit by their own undiscovered talents. At the same time each student is seeing, in his or her own terms, how complex audience response can be and learning how to deal with that complexity in a relatively safe but also demanding environment.

English 101/102 has several other features worth mentioning. Grades are not assigned at the end of the first term; nor are they assigned to individual writings. Instructors often keep assignment-by-assignment records of their students' work and will estimate a provisional grade for students who want to know. By putting grades into what we consider a proper perspective, we feel that we are able to help our students focus their attention fully on the real work of the course. Also in an effort to focus our students' attention on writing we make relatively little use of essay collections. The texts for the course are the writings the students produce. Matters of mechanics, and in fact all matters of form, are handled solely in terms of how they bear on the effectiveness as a communication of the particular piece of writing under discussion. How, the question goes, does the grammar, punctuation, spelling, layout, or typography of this paper enhance or frustrate its intentions toward us as readers? Similarly, our emphasis on the ways form develops out of a relationship between authorial purpose, audience, and subject makes it natural for our students to explore verbal forms outside exposition—fiction, drama, poetry, even writing to be used for speeches or for the making of films. We encourage such exploration and find that it helps enrich our students' sense of the resources a writer has no matter what the particular writing task or style happens to be.

English 101/102 has been a splendid success. A survey done by the department in 1974 showed not only that students looking back at their experience a year or more later felt the course had helped them improve their writing substantially but that they had enjoyed the course as well and looked back on it as a rich part of their first year at the university, significant for them both as a writing course and as an exemplary instance of the kinds of challenges, stimulation, and substance they wanted the university to give them. They did not, definitely, think of 101/102 as a service course, as something to be gotten through or over. Our faculty members show similar enthusiasm; a remarkable number voluntarily teach the course regularly. Such evidence of enthusiasm is the more significant because a faculty member who volunteers to teach 101/102 is committing one third of his or her course load to freshman composition. Both students and teachers also evidence their enthusiasm for the course by doing extra course work in writing. Students regularly sign up for tutorial credits in the term following the conclusion of 101/102, to finish extended writing projects they have been working on or simply to continue their work on writing in the same congenial atmosphere they have been in for the past two terms. Faculty members give extra time to these tutorials, which often have a considerable amount of reading connected with them. The course staff, both graduate assistants and regular faculty, has also voluntarily fielded a set of third-term group tutorials centering on special writing topics such as research-paper writing, poetry writing, and writing on dance. Taking 101/102 also leads students into our creative writing courses, especially into a new course, English 226, "Introduction to Creative Writing," or into English 230, "Non-Fictional Imaginative Prose Writing," a course in the writing of biography, autobiography, and personal essays.

English 101/102 has been an influential course, as the discussion of English 213, our largest composition course, will show. The influence of 101/102 can also be seen in the experimental three-term sequence in scientific writing developed by the department of English in collaboration with the departments of chemistry and physics. This program, now in its fourth year and currently enrolling eighty students, provides an alternate freshman composition sequence for students planning to major in the natural sciences. The first course in the sequence is a general writing course; emphasis on scientific writing comes only in the latter part of the course. Like 101/102, the first term of the sequence concentrates on helping each student learn to write skillfully from a personal perspective and in his own personal voice. The writing of an autobiography of the student's development as a scientist is the major concluding assignment of the first term and neatly integrates the personal and professional emphases of the course. In the second course of the sequence, "The Scientist as Writer," attention focuses on the wide range of writing scientists actually do. Students read a good deal of professional writing by scientists—from Watson and Crick's original article on DNA in *Nature* (as well as selections from *The Double Helix*) to personal essays and fiction by and about scientists. Writing assignments emphasize personal voice and are built around concrete "authentic" writing situations. They are also somewhat more "objective" than those of the first term. Students write, for instance, a profile of a local scientist they have interviewed. In the third course, "Scientific Writing," focus is on the writing of what the course description calls "functional" prose, professional scientific writing in the conventional sense. The third course continues to emphasize the possibility of personal voice even in the more business-like writing the students must do.

The sequence is an exciting one because it is thoroughly practical in its emphasis on helping the science majors enrolled in it become aware of, and good at, the kinds of writing tasks they will actually have to do and because it demonstrates the essential relationship between scientific knowledge and writing ability. The course works from the assumption that the language forms of science have an effect on people's conception of science; thus, language is, on the deepest possible level, as important to the scientist as to the poet. Students like the course because it is both practical and intellectually challenging, and the faculty members and graduate students who teach in the sequence like it for the same reasons. Staff members have recently completed a systematic statistical and qualitative assessment of the sequence with the help of the MSU Office of Learning and Evaluation Services. The assessment has verified staff feeling that the sequence is very successful in helping the students make substantial improvement in their writing.

English 213, the sophomore writing workshop, which is our department's largest composition course, has also been influenced greatly by 101/102 even though it is a substantially different kind of composition course: its aims are different in significant ways, its audience is different, and it has quite a different history. Nothing more need be said about the history of the course except what can always be said: like all courses, English 213 has evolved; it has found its identity through the students, the teachers, and the institution.

Three conditions have significantly shaped the identity of English 213 as a course. First, the course may be taken only by sophomores, juniors, or seniors; it is not open to freshmen, who fulfill their basic university composition requirement in other courses. Second, the students in any particular section of the course are likely to be from a great many different academic programs. Third, students may take the course, as enrollments and their schedules allow, anywhere between their fourth and their last term on campus. As a result of these three conditions, a typical section of English 213 is even more diverse than a comparable freshman composition class would be. The diversity has, moreover, a particular style to it. Writing teachers have long known that older students—veterans and transfer students for instance—tend to be better writers than their eighteen-year-old classmates simply because they are older. They appear to be more adept at taking part in class, at talking to teachers, even—it is often noted—at having ideas and experiences to write about. In a section of English 213 all twenty students are going to have that extra panache, in however mild a form. And it is going to be the stronger because it is a common feature of their situation and because they are not in the course simply to fulfill a requirement in their degree program.

As a result of the characteristics I have just described and through the influence English 101/102 has had on 213, a typical, though by no means universal, way of teaching the course is to concentrate on making students more conscious of themselves as writers and to spend a great deal of class time on student discussion of student writing. In a period of eight or nine weeks, with the class scheduled to meet for no more than three hours per week, students can expect to make substantial progress toward a masterful prose style only if they come into the course with considerable writing experience and considerable knowledge of their own strengths and weaknesses as writers. At the other extreme, a student who comes into the course with little recent writing experience and no great concern to develop as a writer must—in that same time span—be helped, first, to become aware of how he or she performs as a writer and, then, to use that knowledge to improve. It has been our experience, again acknowledging the variety of approaches used by our staff, that working to make students self-aware as writers and spending a good deal of class time on student discussion and editing of papers are very useful ways of succeeding with the diverse and experienced students we encounter in English 213. Even the least interested junior, whose academic program requires little writing, has sufficient writing experience, if only in note-taking, to be able to begin to look at his or her style as a writer and then to experiment with and exercise that style through having it exposed to a sympathetic but also demanding audience.

The emphases I have been describing as characteristic of English 213 have had to be general ones because the course has not been reduced to a common syllabus. Such reduction would violate our sense of how complex the act of teaching is, how diverse the students we teach are, and how complex writing and writing development are. We do not wish to achieve a merely mechanical homogeneity. We also do not wish to let the course be simply whatever the people involved in it at a particular moment or in a particular context think it ought to be. No course can be strong or defensible unless its identity can be communicated. To help articulate the identity of 213 and respect its complexity, we are currently organizing an ambitious and exciting experiment. We plan to develop a set, or "family," of alternate models for English 213. These alternate models will be devised and taught by teams of staff members in which faculty and graduate assistants work together. We are excited about our experiment because we think it will help us fashion an identity for the course that is communicable, replicable, and at the same time answerable to the complexity of the task and to the real possibilities of valid alternate approaches. Equally important, we can use the models to improve our own teaching of the course. Model design can help us see what is going right or wrong in our teaching, and it will give us clues about why. The models will, in addition, help us to communicate with each other, with our students, and with everyone else who is, for whatever reason, interested in the teaching of writing. We think that our experiment will also increase the value of the time and energy that graduate students devote to teaching. Because they will be members of the groups that develop and work on the models, our graduate students will be teaching in a setting that does not isolate them, but instead supports and enriches their experience as teachers. They will, moreover, be doing staff work of more sophistication, interest, and pertinence than they might normally do were they simply assigned to teach two sections of 213. At the end of their graduate career, they will have considerably more valuable experience in the field of writing pedagogy than they could get from several years of isolated, unguided teaching. Our family of models for English 213 will be rich because of its multiplicity, because it will benefit from the particular teaching talents of several persons, and because it is intended to be in a state of continuous refinement. It will be the more valuable because it will help our graduate students, and us, develop as teachers of writing.

TV English in the Dallas County Community College District

Dee Brock, Director of TV English 101

Department responsible for the composition program
   Communications Division of each DCCCD campus
Full-time faculty
   TV English is a part-time assignment for every instructor involved. Some TV
      English instructors are full-time faculty members on one of the DCCCD
      campuses and teach TV English as an overload.
Enrollment policies
   Maximum Enrollment   40
   Minimum Enrollment   20
   Average Enrollment   30
Staffing
   Percentage of TV English courses taught by part-time faculty   50
   Percentage taught by full-time faculty teaching an overload   50
Program size
   500–800 students per semester

Although Dallas County Community College District is a multi-campus district with four strategically placed colleges to serve its community, there is still an unserved group within the roughly one-and-a-quarter million population in the county. Three new campuses soon will help put a college within the reach of all citizens, but there will still be those whose needs cannot be met on campuses: those who are homebound with family responsibilities, those who are ill or injured, those who work erratic schedules or swing shifts, those who are timid about returning to school after years away, those who find the classes or the sections they want already full on campus, those who do not have transportation of their own and are not served by public transportation to the colleges. For these students, the district began offering college-credit open-circuit television instruction in 1972. In 1974, "Writing for a Reason," a college-credit television course, went on the air and became a viable option in the freshman composition program of each district college.

Television students enroll at one of the district colleges, and they are in every sense students of that college. They take tests there; they receive credit there. But their core instruction comes to them in their own homes via the local PBS television channel. Enrollments across the district have ranged from 493 to 826 each semester.

Interestingly, despite the large enrollments in the telecourse, there has been no decline in enrollment in on-campus composition classes. These continue to grow at least as rapidly as the other required courses on campus, and every section offered has "made" on all campuses. Television has simply expanded the opportunities for taking freshman composition to persons who might not have been able to enroll otherwise.

"Writing for a Reason" contains thirty half-hour telelessons. Two lessons are shown each week, and each lesson is repeated three times. If students need to make up or review, they can see lessons on videocassettes in the Learning Resources Centers on any DCCCD college campus.

As the title implies, "Writing for a Reason" has a pragmatic base. Students who enroll are, as a whole, "older" students—the biggest block of them in their thirties. Most of them are employed full or part time; most want to graduate from college; most want additional education in order to earn a raise or a promotion or to get a different job altogether. The course is tailored to this audience; it takes the practical approach that writing is a skill, a skill needed in college and in jobs requiring college training. The course aims to teach students how to handle the real writing problems they are likely to meet in other college courses and in many job situations.

The main goal of "Writing for a Reason" is that students learn to write so effectively that they can fulfill their reasons for writing in college and elsewhere. Consequently, the course covers basic writing skills, such as choosing and shaping a thesis; planning a composition; and composing unified, complete, orderly, and coherent sentences, paragraphs, and essays. Because good writing begins with good thinking, the course gives attention to straight thinking and logic. Because language is the basic medium for all writing, the course covers the high points about the way language functions historically, socially, and psychologically. Mechanics, usage, and grammar are not a part of either the telelessons or the *Study Guide*, but the student receives individual help for his own special problems from his writing consultant. Other goals involve the student's knowing himself better, experiencing his environment more fully, and appreciating his language as a flexible process over which he can have control and through which he can, at least in part, control his world.

The thirty lessons include "The Beginning," a preview of the course; "Language Options," one way to deal with the issues of the students' rights to their own language and standard English or edited English as the dialect of the written word; "The Nature of Communication"; "Readiness," prewriting concerns, especially audience and persona. There are five lessons on the paragraph (a general view and a lesson each on unity, order, completeness, and coherence) and three on the organization of the essay (one lesson on the essay in general, one on introductions, and one on conclusions and transitional paragraphs). Two lessons concentrate on diction; two concentrate on sentences. Nine lessons deal with specific reasons for writing: the paper of definition, the paper of comparison; the paper of classification, the paper of analysis; the letter of application; the essay test; the report; the persuasive essay; and the evaluative essay. Bravely, one lesson covers the history of the English language, and another two cover epistemology, logic, and fallacious reasoning. Naturally, there is a lesson on the dictionary, and using the library is part of the lesson on classification. The last lesson is called "Style."

Although this run-down sounds very traditional, even stodgy, the television lessons are anything but that. Though densely packed with information, they are very entertaining, as six semesters of student evaluations assert. Taking advantage of the television medium, the lessons involve dramatizations, music, celebrities, cartoons, pantomimes, graphics, sight gags, and real people with real reasons for writing. All of the segments are carefully edited, and each lesson is strictly timed; the result is a smoothly paced, interestingly varied program.

The telelesson is only one of the instructional elements. To get full benefit from the course, students must work through each lesson with their *Study Guide*. Each lesson in the *Guide* includes an overview, learning objectives, a pre-test, focus questions that outline major points on the TV program, vocabulary, study exercises, reinforcement of major points, supplementary material, enrichment exercises, a post-test, and, in twelve of the lessons, a mail-in assignment. Each mail-in assignment includes at least one annotated student essay, a step-by-step procedure for writing the paper, and a checklist for the students to use before they mail in their papers.

"Writing for a Reason" is a rigorous composition course, demanding of both faculty and students. The students write something for practice every day and something for the teacher's evaluation every week. Four of the essays are written on campus under controlled conditions—diagnostic papers written during the orientation meeting and three essays that are the major parts of the three tests. In addition, four short papers concentrating on audience and persona, unity, completeness, and coherence are mailed in during the first third of the course. During the last two thirds, the students write seven 500-to-750-word papers. The first four represent particular rhetorical modes—definition, comparison-contrast, classification, and analysis. Then students are asked to use the most effective mode or combination of modes in three other papers: a report, a persuasive essay, and an evaluative essay.

Most of these papers are mailed to consultants, who grade them and mail them back. In order to simplify this process and to ensure that both students and consultants will have copies of the compositions and the comments available for telephone conferences, the students purchase special self-carbon paper in their college bookstore for their mail-in assignments. This paper has two-inch margins on the left side and four-inch margins on the bottom so that the teacher has plenty of space to write comments. These sheets are printed with the address of the college in which the student is enrolled; they also have a place for the student to attach a self-addressed mailing label so that both students and teachers are saved a good deal of time in addressing and stuffing envelopes.

The question of cheating is frequently raised. When someone asks, "How do you know the students don't get someone else to write their papers?" we can only say that we do not really know in all cases. On the other hand, unless all writing is done in class, neither does any other teacher. Even then, diligent students can cheat if they put themselves to the task.

Our control of cheating rests primarily on comparison of the in-class essays (the writing sample at the required orientation and the three essays written under controlled circumstances during the tests) with the rest of each student's work. We also count on the integrity of the students and the expertise of the consultants. Like most college teachers, we find cheating a concern but not an insurmountable problem.

Although there is an on-camera instructor, the on-campus instructors, called writing consultants, are the students' personal teachers. "Writing consultants," by the way, is not just a euphemism. These persons are not mere "graders"; they consult individually with students about their compositions. The writing consultants in DCCCD are either full-time or part-time English faculty at one of the colleges; as such they all have at least a master's degree and some professional teaching experience. Usually about one half of the twenty to twenty-five consultants are full-time faculty.

Each "Writing for a Reason" section "makes" at twenty students and is "full" at twenty-five. The instructor receives the same compensation for this section of twenty to twenty-five students that he would receive for any extra service class. However, if there is a need, the class may be overloaded up to forty students; in this case, the instructor is paid an additional per-student fee for each one above twenty-five. The numbers of students in the sections and the additional fees are based on the results of a time study done during the second semester the course was in operation. Consultants were asked to keep accurate records of what they did and how much time it took them to do it during three specified weeks of the semester. Not all reported on the same three weeks, but each week had several respondents. In addition, each instructor and supervisor was asked to note, on the basis of his or her own experience as well as the results of student surveys, what else a good consultant should do if conditions were ideal. This same kind of study was conducted for all telecourses in an effort to make payment equitable between one discipline and another and between those who worked with television and those who worked with on-campus classes. Even more important was the concern that teachers give their best efforts to the TV students, a demand we did not feel we could make without adequate compensation.

Choosing the writing consultants is the most important job in managing

"Writing for a Reason," for not every good teacher of composition makes a good writing consultant. Being a consultant calls for the same kind of student-centered educational philosophy that DCCCD campuses practice as a whole, but the job calls for other skills and attitudes as well. Whereas the classroom teacher can often be disorganized and unpunctual and still be quite effective because his personality, teaching skills, and physical presence make a positive impact on his students, the good consultant must be quite disciplined. He must keep his office hours strictly, return his phone calls quickly, and grade and remail papers promptly. Necessarily, consultants write longer, more detailed, more coherent, and more legible comments on telecourse papers than they do on other student papers, for the chances are that the students and the writing consultants may know one another only through the written word.

Strangely, some teachers of writing object that there is no interpersonal relationship between students and teachers if there is only writing involved. Actually, being a consultant offers an instructor the opportunity to teach in the kind of one-to-one relationship that most say they want. And those who serve as consultants maintain that the nature of their duties forces them to be better writers and more objective evaluators than other composition-teaching models demand. However, the consultant must be able to find satisfaction in seeing the student's skills improve without necessarily seeing the student's appreciation of the consultant's help grow. While most consultants see their students or talk to them on the phone, they must be willing to handle their function by mail if need be.

In the spring of 1974 when the decision was made to create such a telecourse, there were some doubts whether or not this subject was suited to television. One major objection was the idea that a composition teacher should work with students as they write. Some thought television too impersonal for the kind of human values and personal support that writing classes at their best foster. Others thought that writing, which means putting words on paper, is not visually interesting in itself.

The major objections raised at the beginning were largely overcome in the creation of the course. "Writing for a Reason" does manage to make the subject of composition visually attractive. The course is not impersonal at all; the students relate strongly (and usually positively) to the teacher on camera. The successful students also have a very satisfying one-to-one relationship with their writing consultants, from whom they get more personalized advice about their writing needs than most freshmen receive. There is a good deal of writing in the course, and the students do get personalized evaluations. Further, the research studies have clearly demonstrated that the course does help students improve their composition skills.

Three research studies to evaluate gains in writing skills have been completed: one during each of the first two semesters the course was offered; and one during the spring semester of 1976. Patterned loosely on Arthur Cohen's *Is Anybody Learning to Write?*—a national study to assess writing—the design in each case called for entry and exit writing samples for each student under controlled circumstances. The third study also included twelve on-campus classes as control groups. Two predetermined topics were used in each case. Half of the students wrote on Topic *A* at the beginning and on Topic *B* at the end; the others used the reverse order. After the papers were coded so that they could be identified without revealing either the students' identities or the dates the papers were written, fifty pairs of papers from each semester of TV students and, in the last study, fifty pairs from the control classes were randomly selected for reading. Four composition instructors (one from each of the DCCCD campuses) who had had no involvement with the telecourse were the evaluators. Each paper was read at least twice; if there was a significant variance in scores, the paper was read by a third reader. The papers first received a holistic score. Then they were judged for their excellence in seven areas: content development, organization of the complete paper, paragraphing, diction, sentences, usage, and mechanics. All three studies were conducted in a similar way. All three studies showed significant student gains in all categories, whether the course was taught on campus or via television. The most significant gains, however, were on the telecourse papers in the areas on which "Writing for a Reason" places the most emphasis: organization and development of the complete paper, organization and development of individual paragraphs, and holistic scores.

In addition, a follow-up study of students who took composition via "Writing for a Reason" shows that their successful completion rate in the second semester of freshman composition is identical with that of students who took the first-semester composition course on a DCCCD campus. The only significant difference revealed by this research was that a higher percentage of former TV students than on-campus students made As in their second-semester composition class.

Student course evaluations in the form of anonymous questionnaires have been used at various times and at the final test each semester. The attitudes are clearly positive. On a scale of one to five (with five high) the overall course average is 3.9. Certain elements of the course consistently rank much higher.

Yet we are not without problems. The major one is student participation. The course calls for enormous self-discipline on the part of the students, who must watch the programs, do their work, mail in their assignments by themselves. Neither the rewards nor the anxieties of the classroom with peers and instructor spur them on. Of those who enrolled in the first fall semester, twenty-six percent were never heard from again. They paid their tuition and disappeared; only sixty-five percent of those enrolled took the first test. While the situation has improved, many students still drop out. What happens to those students? We are still trying to find out. Our mail-out survey did not elicit much response. (Apparently if the students did not want to mail in assignments, they did not want to mail back a survey either.) Telephone surveys garnered more data. Students generally said they had not realized how much time the course would take or how little time they would have to give to it. Or they said they had new jobs, new mates, or personal or family illnesses and problems. At any rate, at the end of the first semester, fifty-five percent of those who had sent in at least one assignment completed the course with a passing grade and earned their three hours of credit. The completion rates for the total enrollments have ranged from forty to sixty percent.

"Writing for a Reason" is also used as an on-campus, individualized instruction package. In this mode the students are allowed flexible entry; they can enroll any Monday there is an opening in the class. Although there is a limit to the amount of time they may use to complete the course, they are free to pace themselves within this frame to suit their own schedules and abilities. Preliminary research on the first experimental sections shows significant student gains in writing skills and has encouraged each of the district campuses to use the course as an on-campus option.

As a useful spin-off for the district, individual lessons from "Writing for a Reason" have found favor with many of the composition instructors. They use their favorites in the same ways they use supplementary films within the typical classroom format.

"Writing for a Reason" cost about eighty-five thousand dollars to develop, a mere pittance in the realm of television production, but rather steep for college course development by other standards. However, with its steady enrollment within DCCCD and its lease or purchase fees from the hundred colleges and universities in the United States and Canada that use it, "Writing for a Reason" has been a good investment for DCCCD and remains a popular and effective option for the freshman composition program.

The Writing Adjunct Program at the Small College of California State College, Dominguez Hills

Marilyn Sutton, Director of the Writing Adjunct Program

Because of the special nature of the writing adjunct program, the information preceding the other essays in this volume is not pertinent here.

Quite unlike the other reports in this volume, most of which describe a complete freshman composition program on an individual campus, the following description presents a particular approach to the teaching of composition at any point in the college curriculum, an approach that was developed at the Small College on the Dominguez Hills campus of the California State system[1] and later extended to several campuses. Established in 1972, with support from the Carnegie Corporation and the Division of New Program Development and Evaluation within the CSUC, the Small College was charged with developing alternatives within the instructional process that could be of value to other colleges. One such alternative is the writing adjunct, an individualized composition course offered in conjunction with courses in other subject areas. Originating quite naturally from the interdisciplinary nature of the Small College, the writing adjunct was judged by faculty and students alike to be a highly successful vehicle for the teaching of writing. In 1975–76, a multi-campus proposal for transferring the program to other interested campuses was granted funding, and the following year additional funding was awarded to extend the program still further. By 1976–77, nine California State campuses had tested writing adjunct programs, an additional three had developed adjunct-like programs, and faculty on approximately forty campuses spread throughout the country had requested program materials with an eye to considering the suitability of the writing adjunct program for their campuses.

Since the writing adjunct program crosses departmental lines and deviates from standard class-hour formulas, a detailed discussion of the logistics of the program is a useful preface to general comments on the program itself.

Registration

Students register in both a subject-matter course (those courses that offer possible links with the writing adjunct are flagged in the class schedule), and in the writing adjunct course. Since the writing adjunct is identified as a separate course from the outset, many of the problems of optional writing labs are overcome. It is clear from the beginning that the writing adjunct carries a distinct course content in composition and that the writing adjunct instructor will be responsible for determining the syllabus in composition and evaluating each student's progress as a writer.

Diagnosis

At a first interview, students are requested to present a recent sample of their writing and to complete a brief diagnostic grammar test. Then each student is asked to consider what he or she might gain from a course in composition and to suggest a number of goals that could be set for the term. With each student involved in establishing his or her own goals, students begin to consider the process of writing as well as the final product and are encouraged to think of themselves as writers—something quite unusual for them—and the composition course as an experience that might actually help them.

Drafting and Revising

Students regularly submit their first drafts to the writing adjunct program, usually at least one week before the paper is due in the subject-matter course.

All drafts are read twice; once by a writing tutor and once by a writing adjunct instructor. Each reader responds to the draft by making suggestions for improvement instead of corrections. Either the instructor or the tutor then meets with the student for a paper conference, for when the student meets with a qualified professional over a piece of the student's own writing, the hopes of teaching writing are best realized. The student leaves the conference armed with the responses of two readers and convinced that revision is necessary as much to clarify his or her thoughts as to meet standards of correctness.

One quite subordinate, but nevertheless significant, by-product of this process is that opportunities for plagiarism shrink. When the revisions are completed, the student prepares two copies of the final paper: one for submission to the instructor in the subject-matter class, the other to the writing adjunct instructor, who will place it in the student's file to serve as a partial basis for evaluating the student's progress in composition.

The writing adjunct is more a structure for the teaching of composition than a particular course content, and as such, is highly flexible. The composition program of the Small College is built entirely on the writing adjunct model, but more often, the writing adjunct is found as an option within, or as a particular level of, a varied composition program. The writing adjunct format has been used to structure composition programs at the freshman level, at the graduate level, and even at the "remedial" level; but typically it has been used to structure composition offerings at the sophomore or junior level. It is the versatility of the structure, as well as the assumptions about the teaching of writing that underlie that structure (most important of which is the belief that the teaching of writing should find a central position in the college curriculum), that makes the writing adjunct a well-suited response to several challenges that are facing the CSUC system in the mid-seventies.

In 1975, when the multi-campus project was first funded, composition teachers in California faced several challenges. The first challenge was the responsibility of working with the new student populations in the California State system; these populations were entering with a wide diversity of backgrounds (socioeconomic as well as linguistic), of prior writing preparation, and of current writing proficiency. The writing adjunct's capacity to provide individual diagnosis and prescription for students, together with its use of tutorial instruction, offered a viable method of responding to the widely differing needs of the students.

A second challenge, and one with a discouragingly lengthy tradition, was that students usually regarded any composition course as a hurdle set out by the university rather than as an educational pursuit of any direct value to themselves. Even more often, students affected what is sometimes described as the "innoculation theory" of education: the belief that once the composition requirement has been met, no reason remains for improving, or even maintaining, their writing ability. Instructing through assignments given in regular college courses (often courses in the students' major), the writing adjunct meets this challenge by drawing not only on the students' desire to "do well" in those courses, but on the truism that students write best when they have something to say. Students in the adjunct program write on topics related to courses they have selected for study. Thus, the course lectures, class discussions, and assigned reading in the subject-matter course all serve to put the student in an informed position for writing: much of the work of prewriting is complete by the beginning of the first draft. Since the writing adjunct course is usually repeatable, each occasion being grounded on goals of increasing sophistication, the structure enables continued reinforcement of the composition teacher's effort and fosters the notion that effective communication is a lifelong as well as a college-wide task.

A third challenge developed from the renewed discussion about which sector of the university should be responsible for the teaching of writing. The size of the task indicated that the efforts of more than one department were needed; further, some faculty members questioned whether any one department was sufficiently catholic in its approach, yet specialized in its knowledge, to teach writing for all disciplines. When faculty in all disciplines were asked to teach composition within each of their courses, they often found themselves frustrated in the resulting impossibility of treating the primary subject matter thoroughly and, in fact, they frequently found themselves working from a weak base of expertise (for the literacy crisis, if it exists, is surely a second-generation crisis). The division of labor in the writing adjunct program solves this problem because it renders hopes of shared responsibility genuinely possible: the adjunct instructor, a composition specialist, establishes writing goals with the students, conducts the instruction in composition, and evaluates student progress in composition; the subject-matter faculty member, a specialist in a particular discipline, designs topics for writing assignments and builds solid writing requirements into the syllabus of the course in the subject area, all the while assured that students will have instruction in composition that can be applied in fulfilling the required writing assignments.

Even though the writing adjunct offers a structural response to challenges rather than a particular course content, it does proceed from a set of assumptions: specifically that writing can be taught—that there is a *technique of writing* that can be transmitted if the student is actively engaged in the writing process; that students are greatly encouraged to learn when they perceive the connection between their work in composition and their work in other areas; that the process of drafting and revising lies at the heart of the composing process; that heterogeneous student needs are best answered by a composition program that employs several instructional modes; that the goal of creating a literate student population is best served by a faculty who establish shared values and standards as well as shared responsibility in the teaching of writing and that, to be effective, a program based on shared responsibilities must clearly define the roles of involved faculty; and finally, that writing ought to be an integral part—an "enabling discipline" in the words of Richard Larson[2]—of the undergraduate curriculum as opposed to a rather isolated one- or two-term sequence reserved for freshmen.

From these assumptions and the needs displayed in the CSUC system in the early seventies, a set of course components evolved. Each writing adjunct course, regardless of its position in a particular composition sequence, begins with the writing instructor making an analysis of each student's writing strengths and weaknesses. The student is then encouraged—indeed, required in most instances—to take part in establishing goals that will serve as the basis for individualized writing assignments given throughout the term. In addition to the individualized program of study, each student will also meet weekly in class session for presentations of composition topics of general applicability. The heart of the program, however, remains the drafting and revising of papers assigned by other subject-matter courses. For it is in revising a first draft that a student can bring the theory and practice of composition together with study in other areas. The process of drafting and revising (and, if necessary, additional revising), is repeated as many times as the student has papers assigned by the subject-matter instructor in a given term. Near the close of the term, students meet together in small editing workshops to exchange papers and analyze them, offering suggestions for revision. This editing exercise puts the student in the position of the writing tutor, and besides cultivating a healthy respect for writing tutors, continues the training of the student as editor, and ultimately as self-editor.

On campuses where the writing adjunct is employed as an alternative to a required freshman-composition sequence, all individual writing goals are established within the context of the objectives for the campus composition requirement. During the initial sessions, students who appear unlikely to meet the requirement within one term are advised to replace the writing adjunct course or to supplement it with work in the campus center for basic skills instruction. On the other hand, students whose written proficiency at the time of the initial screening appears adequate to the campus competencies are advised to "challenge" the requirement by submitting a portfolio representing a range of writing ability to a panel of three composition instructors, each of whom will make an evaluation and a recommendation regarding the awarding of credit.

On campuses where the writing adjunct has been established as a repeatable mini-course, students are encouraged to see that their growth in writing ability should, and can, keep pace with their overall education. On these campuses, even very good writers, a small but increasingly neglected population, can be admitted to the adjunct program and work on goals of a more sophisticated nature.

The strongly individualized nature of the writing adjunct program lends itself quite naturally to the use of tutors. Deciding whether or not to employ tutors in an undergraduate program generally involves such a complex of forces (at the least, pedagogic, ethical, and budgetary factors) that in all cases, the decision was left to the individual campuses developing adjunct programs. The Small College program has incorporated the use of peer tutors who are carefully screened and then trained in a special course titled "Peer Tutoring in Writing." As part of their course requirement, the tutors meet regularly with students, assist with composition assignments when students need additional help, and serve as first readers on all student drafts. Defining the tasks of the tutor in this fashion relieves the peer tutor of responsibilities that seem inappropriate—e.g., grading and making ultimate judgments on student papers—and frees the tutor to serve where he or she is most effective, i.e., as an interested and informed audience for the student writer. The evaluations of the experience of tutoring in the adjunct program have included student attitude questionnaires, faculty evaluation-reports, weekly reports by tutors, and a final attitude questionnaire for tutors: all have been highly favorable, and it is not surprising that both faculty and tutors have noted that tutoring has a positive effect on the tutor's own writing.

Each of the other campuses employing the writing adjunct format decided to build a role for tutors into the program, though the methods for selecting, training and compensating tutors have varied widely. Common to each experience has been the conviction that there are some things in the teaching of writing that tutors do more effectively than instructors—perhaps because students can see tutors as writing coaches more easily than they can instructors—but that great care must be exercised in selecting the tutors and in defining their functions, particularly if the tutors have had little formal training in the teaching of writing. In the adjunct program, some difficulties normally associated with the use of tutors have been averted because of the existence of a special manual for peer tutors working in writing adjunct programs and an individualized resource index that codes writing problems to appropriate sources.

On the campuses involved in the multi-campus writing adjunct project, and on those campuses where faculty requested materials for the program, the greatest value of the program is likely to lie in its catalytic effect on plans for redirecting the teaching of writing from a departmental home and responsibility to a more central position in the college curriculum, for creating a campus-wide forum for discussing the skills and standards of literacy, and for encouraging students to think of themselves as writers and to realize that the goal of writing well is not a luxury reserved for the English major (English departments have, of course, always known this), but a realistic possibility for all undergraduates. It is in offering a practical framework for reinforcing writing skills, particularly at the sophomore and junior levels, and for enlisting campus-wide support in that effort that the writing adjunct is most likely to be found in the future within the California State sysem.

Notes

[1] The California State Universities and Colleges, one of two state university systems in California, comprises 19 campuses; the University of California includes 9 campuses.

[2] Richard L. Larson, "English: An Enabling Discipline," *ADE Bulletin*, No. 6 (Sept. 1975), p. 3.

Functional Writing at Brown University

A. D. Van Nostrand, Chairman of the English Department

Department responsible for the composition program   English
Full-time faculty in the department   45
Enrollment policies
    Maximum Enrollment   25
    Minimum Enrollment   None
    Average Enrollment   25
Staffing
    Percentage of freshman composition courses taught by graduate students   90
    Percentage taught by assistant, associate, and/or full professors   10
Program size
    Number of students enrolled in the freshman composition program in the fall term of 1976   319
    Number of sections of freshman composition offered in the fall term of 1976   11
    Number of sections at all levels—literature, composition, film, graduate, undergraduate, etc.—offered by the department in the fall term of 1976   114

The English composition requirement at Brown reads as follows:

> Competence in reading and writing the English language is re-
> quired for all degrees.
>
> In general, it is expected that such competence will have been
> demonstrated prior to entrance. . . . Those students who, in the
> opinion of the Dean, have not clearly demonstrated such com-
> petence must enroll in English 1 for course credit in their first
> semester.
>
> All students are expected to continue to demonstrate compe-
> tence in reading and writing English during the period of their
> degree candidacy. Students who, in the opinion of any of their in-
> structors, fail to do so will be referred to the Dean and may be re-
> quired to enroll in English 1.

English 1 itself is a course in functional writing, intended primarily for
freshmen but open to anyone at any class level. Enrollment is optional in all
but a few cases. The course is presented in an individualized format designed
for one semester, but a student can use up to five weeks of a second semester
to complete a contract. Students write about five thousand words in assigned
papers and about six thousand words in connection with *Functional Writing*,
a text/workbook.[1]

The text is about building relationships in paragraphs and paragraph-
sequences. Its major characteristics are its instructional format and the theory
of writing that it presents. They are related to one another in a kind of organic
form: the book does what it says. This relationship between a theory of
rhetoric and an instructional format has a history, parts of which are printed
elsewhere. My remarks here draw largely on these sources.[2]

The Theory

As in many other colleges and universities, the students who arrived at
Brown in the early seventies had conditioned themselves to verbalize without
recourse to writing. Consisting of themes and grammar, schoolroom writing
bore almost no relation to the way students formed their thoughts. They had
been taught repeatedly to acknowledge their writing problems, but they had
never been taught how to overcome them. After years of being graded by
standards that were often incomprehensible, almost all the freshmen at Brown
carried with them an attitude toward writing that had, in fact, become the
most important part of the problem. The problem of the students' writing
ability and their attitude toward writing was, moreover, exacerbated by a
system of writing instruction that had been prevalent in universities for more
than fifteen years: the freshmen were turned over to graduate students, who
had little or no training in teaching writing and who in some cases even
suffered the same separation of verbalizing from formal discourse that limited
their students. The graduate students themselves, of course, aspired to teach
literature, not writing; thus, it was easy for them to rationalize their own
inabilities. In sum, we found at Brown those negative attitudes that were
commonly institutionalized in the national endeavor to teach freshmen how to
write.

Something was needed to give instructors confidence while they were teaching. Some system was needed for informing both parties, teacher and student, even as classes were in progress. Designing a system to satisfy this dual purpose depended on making the instruction sequential, so as to guide the instructors as it guided the students, but at a faster pace. The strategy of design was to equip the instructor well enough to explain, at any given time, what the student needed to know.

The first task, then, was to find a way to make a course in writing sequential and therefore cumulative. The second task was to divide the information into units small enough to be dealt with discretely. The members of the task force at Brown decided that the way to accomplish both tasks was to create a course about writing itself—that is, about whatever process goes on when a person writes. If the course of instruction could describe some normative process of writing, then learners could use this norm to measure their own individual habits. They could recognize for themselves those habits that tended to facilitate their writing, as well as those habits that tended to get in the way, and they could modify their habits accordingly. To create such a course we needed an informing theory—some way to explain the phenomena we wanted to present. Though it did not need to be complete to start with, the theory needed to be credible, reasonably predictive, and based on as broad a data set as possible.

I had developed such a theory of writing during seven years of experiment with the writing habits of persons in corporate-management groups—persons who wrote formal discourse daily. Observing what they wrote, as opposed to what they had intended to write, I perceived two processes at work that seemed to be at odds with each other. One was the writer's deliberate attempt to communicate, which caused certain expectations in the reader, that is, a contract for the writer to follow. The other was the writer's process of exploring the subject, learning more about it by writing. This second process often caused the writer to contradict the reader's expectations, breaking the contract. Nevertheless, awareness of the two competing processes allowed us to develop a program of writing instruction based on what we call the "contract theory of writing."

The contract theory of writing explains the normal and conflicting energies of writer and reader in such a way as to enable the reader's expectations to guide the writer's learning process. This seems at first to be paradoxical. In fact, the contract theory of writing *can* be stated as a paradox, thus: *It is easier to organize your information for someone else than it is to organize it for yourself.* Like any paradox, however, this can be explained. The reader's needs are simpler than the writer's—which is why the theory works. At any given moment during the reading process, and with more or less intensity, the reader needs to know the significance of what is being said. The reader asks some form of the question "So what?" This need for assurance is very simple compared to the complexity of the writer's needs. At any given moment during the writing process, the writer is usually trying to solve too many questions of priorities to be aware of the one thing the reader most needs to know, which is "So what?" Learning how to recognize the various forms of the reader's implied question, however, and learning how to accommodate them will speed up the writer's learning process.

The Text

The text/workbook, *Functional Writing*, analyzes the writing process. The book is descriptive, not prescriptive. It shows the writer certain mental operations that are common to all writing, and it illustrates ways of controlling these operations to suit the writer's purpose. These operations are choices that the writer makes in deriving relationships from any set of information, and also choices in selecting new information to support those relationships. Since the writing process is dynamic and repetitive, the writer repeats the choices again, learning as he goes; for the act of writing itself generates knowledge. In short, the book presents the learner with ways of controlling choices: it describes the choices in terms of making assertions, of selecting evidence from sets of information, of inferring a reader's frame of reference, and of using that frame of reference to guide the development of the writer's own organizing idea; at the same time, it explains the necessary tension between the writer's natural groping for something to say and the need to say it in a way that a reader can comprehend. Specifically, the book shows the writer how to use a reader's expectations as a means of guiding his own choices; it provides the writer with a set of workable strategies for writing. Designed as a kind of laboratory in which the learner can apply these strategies, each chapter of the book presents a continuous and graduated set of writing situations and presents a set of objectives for the learner to achieve in applying these strategies. Specifically, the text/workbook shows the learner the properties of an assertion, the function of an organizing idea, and the nature of evidence. It shows the learner how to use these concepts in accommodating the reader's expectations: how to build sequences, how to forecast these sequences, and how to use continuous forecasting to develop a complete statement.

The text is sequential and cumulative. Every chapter appears in the same format. The book can be used alone or with other instructional material, including texts for reading, style manuals, and handbooks for editing. Because the text is sequential, the student can sustain interruptions without having to retrace previous assignments. Because the workbook sections are cumulative, the learner can readily transfer what he or she learns at any stage to other writing activities in other subjects. Because each section of the book is discrete, it is possible for instructors to adapt the pace of instruction to learners who start at different levels of competency. The adaptability of the text was developed through extensive field testing, over a five-year period, at fifteen different sites, including secondary schools, two-year colleges, four-year colleges, and technical institutes. It was used in classrooms and in language laboratories, and students who worked with it represented all levels from grade twelve through graduate courses.

The System of Instruction

Functional Writing is also a system of instruction that reinforces the instructor's primary task, which is the evaluation of writing. Coordinated with each of the mental operations it describes, the text presents a precise definition of standards for evaluating the writer's work, standards that are stated in seven major structural terms, without reference to subject or to what is often called *content*. The structural terms can be referred to any writing sample. Accordingly, the system makes it possible for both the learner and the instructor to speak the same language when they analyze any written statement.

Because it is sequential and cumulative, the text is adapted to group instruction, tutorial instruction, or a mixed mode combining both. Determining the instructional mode is a function of class time, class size, control of attendance, and evaluating procedures available to the instructor. Both group instruction and individualized instruction have limitations and advantages in a writing course. The limitations of either mode tend to be the advantages of the other. Group instruction provides the easiest means of keeping track of everyone in the class, of dispensing information in an orderly way, and of guaranteeing the emphases that the instructor wants to achieve; but it also removes from class time the activity of evaluating each learner's writing, and it necessitates more conference time in office hours. Individualized instruction, on the other hand, allows the instructor to give a detailed, personal evaluation of each piece of writing. At the same time, it reduces competition among learners, who set their own pace, and it reinforces the sense of the learner controlling his or her own achievement. But individualized instruction also taxes the learner's responsibility. Some persons cannot handle indefinite deadlines, and keeping track of such persons can be very time consuming. The alternative, a grade of *Incomplete*, is always costly.

The functional writing system of instruction is conducted differently at different colleges. At Brown, it is conducted by one instructor for every twenty-five students, aided by one or two reviewers in each class. Reviewing consists of reading and discussing with the writer the completed assignments in the workbook and also the test following each chapter of the text. These discussions are guided by sets of questions and answers specified in the instructor's manual, and they accommodate the criteria for evaluating writing that are successively stated in each chapter of the text. The reviewer does not grade a student's work. In the functional writing system, reviewing is a role that can be performed by anyone who has already completed the assignment in question, and who is familiar with the criteria in the text and the guiding questions in the manual. The reviewer can be a student in the course or a graduate of the course. For the person who has just completed a given writing assignment, the reviewer is a live reader who can make informed and candid responses to the writing. And the reviewer, of course, stands to gain in this transaction, by having to convert a passive understanding to an active understanding of the concepts in the text.

The demand that the functional writing system makes lies precisely in the fact that it is a unified model of the writing process. It is not a casual grab bag of rhetorical, logical, and grammatical information. It must be read before it can be taught, which makes it unusual as composition texts go. The argument is holistic and demands intellectual attention from the instructor before it can be adapted to the classroom. *Functional Writing* itself has proven to be an extraordinarily simple book from which to teach, once the teacher understands its line of reasoning, but it can be a problem to the instructor who does not know it as well as the students do—if that instructor takes for granted the conventional assumptions about writing that the book specifically repudiates. *Functional Writing* was built on the premise that many teachers are not qualified by their academic preparation to teach writing. The book requires that they make up the deficiency—by reading it as part of their own education —before they teach with it.

Notes

[1] A. D. Van Nostrand, C. H. Knoblauch, Peter J. McGuire, and Joan Pettigrew, *Functional Writing* (Providence, R.I.: Center for Research in Writing, 1973; Boston: Houghton Mifflin, 1978).

[2] The sources include the *Instructor's Guide to "Functional Writing"* (Boston: Houghton Mifflin, 1978); "English 1 and the Measurement of Writing," *Proceedings of the Second National Conference,* 1975 (Washington, D.C.: Center for Personalized Instruction, 1976); and "A New Direction in Teaching Writing," *Educational Technology,* 17 (Sept. 1977).

The Senior Rhetoric Program in the College of Engineering at the University of Michigan

J. C. Mathes, Chairman, Department of Humanities

Department responsible for the composition program   Humanities
Full-time faculty in the department   27
Enrollment policies
    Maximum Enrollment   17
    Minimum Enrollment   12
    Average Enrollment   16
Staffing
    Percentage of rhetoric courses taught by full-time instructors or lecturers   10
    Percentage taught by assistant, associate, and full professors   90
Program size
    Number of students enrolled in the rhetoric program in the fall term
        of 1976   237
    Number of sections of rhetoric offered in the fall term of 1976   18
    Number of sections at all levels—literature, rhetoric, film, graduate, un-
        dergraduate, etc.—offered by the department in the fall term of 1976   97

The department of humanities in the University of Michigan's College of Engineering primarily provides instruction for undergraduate engineering students, who must take at least twelve of their required twenty-four to thirty hours of humanities and social sciences from the department. The freshman engineering students we serve have the same SAT verbal scores as other freshmen at the university, and they have higher SAT math scores. In addition to those enrolled in the College of Engineering, the department serves on an elective basis both undergraduate and graduate students from other professional schools and from the liberal arts and sciences. The department does offer a degree program in technical and professional communication as an option in the college's interdisciplinary engineering program.

While freshman composition is the traditional approach to teaching writing in college, it is not in fact the only approach. Indeed, our program resulted from a decision that the best way to deal with the problems of teaching writing is to abandon freshman composition altogether and institute a senior-level rhetoric requirement. Thus, the program itself illustrates a true *option* to "freshman" composition and suggests an alternative some schools may wish to consider. The program consists of four courses (3 credit hours each); each engineering senior is required to take *one* of the four. The senior rhetoric courses are "Creative Writing—Fiction, Poetry, Drama"; "Argument and Persuasion"; "Technical and Professional Writing for Industry, Government, and Business"; and "Scientific and Technical Communication." Except for "Creative Writing," multiple sections of all the senior rhetoric courses are offered each term, and all sections are limited to sixteen students. Students not enrolled in the College of Engineering also elect these courses, and engineering students often elect an additional senior rhetoric course.

In addition to the four senior-level courses, the department offers numerous elective writing courses, at least one at each undergraduate level. Any engineering student at the appropriate level (and students from other colleges in the university) may elect one of the following courses: for freshmen, "Composition for Foreign Students" (ESL) or "Writer's Workshop" (a "Personalized System of Instruction" approach to individual writing problems and projects); for sophomores, "Strategies in Writing" (an applied writing or project-oriented course); for juniors, "Theory and Practice of Argument" (public argument, often in debate-team format); and for seniors, "Information Research," "Writing Design Project Reports," and "Oral Presentation" (three different mini-courses, each designed to meet differing professional needs). On the graduate level, the department offers "Internship in Technical and Professional Communication" (for the technical-writing option of the Interdisciplinary Engineering Program), "Advanced Technical and Professional Communication" (for students with actual professional communication tasks on the job or on a research grant) and "Thesis, Dissertation Proposal, and Dissertation Writing for Engineers and Scientists." Each freshman course has two or three sections a term, and the other electives have one section a term. A computer-assisted grammar review laboratory and a university-wide reading and writing improvement service—neither of which carries credit—serve as a support system for all of these courses.

The senior rhetoric program, established in 1968 when the university's freshman composition requirement had been abandoned, was designed to meet objectives entirely different from those that were being addressed by the freshman composition program. The senior-level program resulted from our dissatisfaction with a freshman composition program, which, though it had taken many forms, had failed to improve the writing skills of freshman students. Partially through conscious effort but primarily through gradual accretion, the program has come to focus on three "objectives": enabling students to write well enough to pursue their chosen careers, encouraging them to broaden their intellectual horizons, and, through the first two objectives, teaching them the conventions of "standard literacy." For example, the syllabus for a typical section of "Argument and Persuasion" reads as follows:

> The purpose of this course is to put you in reasonable control of the process of developing persuasive discourse. You will be taught a process of inquiry, a concept of the shape and limits of argument among reasonable people, how to analyze and formulate problems, how to develop an argument of fact and an argument of policy, and methods of selecting, arranging, writing, and editing information on the basis of your intended impact on your intended audiences.

The primary objective of this course is to broaden the intellectual horizon of the students; thus, the course emphasizes rhetorical theory. The syllabus for a typical section of "Technical and Professional Writing for Industry, Government, and Business," on the other hand, describes a rather different course:

> The purpose of this course is to train you in communications of the sort required of practicing engineers and managers on-the-job. Specifically, you will be taught to design technical reports by following a systematic procedure. This procedure will enable you to analyze the audiences for reports, to state the purposes for reports, to select and arrange report materials, and to prepare and edit a report text. In short, the purpose of this course is to improve your mastery of the whole process of report writing from the pre-writing stages through the final editing stages.

The primary objective of this course is to enable students to write well "on-the-job."

Both these courses address the problem of teaching basic literacy—the language skills necessary to express oneself effectively, the skills expected of any "educated" person. Though we assume that our students, as seniors, are literate (and indeed they are quite literate by the usual standards of measure), these courses solve literacy problems by addressing the students' career objectives and by appealing to their intellectual objectives. For example, our career-oriented rhetoric courses teach students how to analyze an audience and to articulate the purpose of a piece of written communication. Our experience convinces us that many literacy problems disappear when a writer has a real purpose for writing. On the other hand, our rhetoric courses with intellectual objectives solve many literacy problems by addressing them as conceptual problems rather than as applied skills problems.

By many indicators—enrollment pressure, student evaluation, faculty evaluation, college satisfaction, employer and alumni response, measured improvement in skills—the senior rhetoric program has proven to be extraordinarily successful, although this has come at some cost and has created new problems. Many students and engineering faculty consider our senior rhetoric course the single most important *engineering* course engineering students take. After graduation many students write or return to tell us how much they appreciate having studied in the senior rhetoric program—something we find extremely gratifying.

The success of our program results primarily from the emphasis on the conceptual and prewriting stages of writing that the career and intellectual objectives require in our rhetoric courses. The success in large measure also results from the mechanical device of shifting the required composition course from the freshman year to the senior year. Seniors have a felt need to improve their communication skills, and thus have a positive attitude toward the composition requirement and apply themselves to improve their skills. They work conscientiously, and they work hard. Seniors also appreciate the sophistication of the primary course objectives, which are cognitive rather than the exclusively applied skills objectives typical of courses focusing primarily on literacy.

Though our senior-level program seems to produce students with the writing skills a college graduate is expected to have acquired, and thereby solves the basic problem that initially motivated the switch to senior rhetoric, at the same time, the program has presented us with other problems. First, we need some method of addressing the problems of basic literacy *before* the senior year. Our data show that the attrition between the freshman and junior years is about fifty percent; thus, by delaying composition until the senior year, we fail to meet the needs of fifty percent of the students who enroll in the College of Engineering. Clearly the senior-level program does no good at all for those students. Moreover, many of us think that a freshman with literacy problems should not have to wait for three years before those problems are addressed. In an attempt to offer help on the freshman level, we have instituted a course entitled "Writer's Workshop," which relies on PSI-modules and tutorial approaches to the teaching of writing. We also have established a noncredit computer-assisted grammar-review lab for students who need training in grammar and mechanics. Whether these approaches will provide a workable solution remains to be determined, because it has taken several years to integrate them into the curriculum. Initial results, however, are promising.

A second problem is that the senior-level program does nothing to help engineering students do well in the courses they take before they are seniors. To succeed in college, a student needs to acquire the cognitive and applied skills of systematic investigation, of stating and documenting a conclusion, and of presenting evidence appropriately and convincingly in term papers, themes, essay exams, lab reports, and the like. We have not found a means of addressing this problem. In 1968 we assumed that the essays in the required freshman-level "great books" course, which replaced the freshman composition requirement, would prove sufficient. By now we realize that requiring writing in a literature course in no way substitutes for the kind of training that once was given in freshman composition. We are now concerned with finding some means of solving this problem.

Despite these two important problems, we think that our writing program is successful. We have developed an effective means of improving the cognitive and applied skills of our students. Our products—the graduating seniors —usually are literate and effective writers and, perhaps as important, have the confidence that they are.